# WHAT PEOPLE ARE SAYING
## ABOUT **40,000 WORDS**
### *about*
## MARRIAGE & PARENTING

There are not always enough words, but my friend Shannon O'Dell has given us 40K of them to get our marriage and parenting on the right track. As I always say, marriage is a workout and as you work out the truths found on each page you will be on the fast track to success in your relationships. The marriage yoke is no joke so take in every word for a more meaningful and beautiful home.

—Pastor Ed Young Jr, Senior Pastor,
Fellowship Church Grapevine TX

Don't allow the 40,000 words to scare you . . . use the tips Shannon offers to help you keep your marriage and parenting rock solid and red-hot!

—David Crank, Senior Pastor/Founder, FaithChurch.com,
St. Louis, MO and West Palm Beach, FL

I believe in Shannon O'Dell and the 40,000 words of this book. He and Cindy have been a great example of what a marriage can be through hard work and sacrifice.

—Brad White, Director of C3 Global, Grapevine, TX

From my first encounter with Shannon, I found him to be creative, innovative, and highly intelligent. He's a person who humbly brought a practical biblical perspective to all we spoke about. I'm glad he's brought that same practical and passionate perspective to the vital subject of marriage.

—David Hughes, Senior Pastor
Church By The Glades, Ft. Lauderdale, FL

Pastor Shannon wants to help you avoid some major landmines in your marriage and family, and he does it with humility and transparency in *40,000 Words About Marriage & Parenting*. He brings the truth forward because of his heart after God and his love for people, and I support that 100%. It's punchy, and it's well worth your time.

—Rick Bezet, Author & Lead Pastor of
New Life Church of Arkansas

Shannon and Cindy have hit it out of the park! 40K Homerun!!! These tremendous leaders and, more than that, a rockstar couple, have shared their secrets to a great marriage. I know this book will impact you and your marriage.

—Troy Maxwell, Senior Pastor Freedom House, Charlotte, NC

This book is not just filled with words that are meaningless; they come from a man who has lived them out with his wife and children. He is able to write from the perspective of walking through these things himself. I'm thankful for the relationship I have with Shannon and the opportunity that you'll get to see his heart on paper and apply it to your life. *40,000 Words About Marriage & Parenting* will not only bless you, but it will impact your marriage and family.

—Tim Chambers, Senior Pastor
Fresh Start, Egg Harbor, NJ

Marriage and parenting are more complex and challenging than ever before. This is why I am thankful that God has raised up a man like Shannon O'Dell to address each of these subjects from a biblical worldview and do it in a straightforward manner. Please get a copy of this book for yourself and another one for a friend.

—Dr. Ronnie W. Floyd
Author, Ministry Strategist, and Pastor Emeritus, Cross Church

If you are looking for straightforward answers to marriage and parenting issues that contain practical advice, you need to get *40,000 Words About Marriage & Parenting* today! Shannon not only provides great insight into the issues of marriage and parenting, he provides life examples, practical applications, and a biblical worldview of family. I highly recommend this book to those who are struggling, but also to those who are teaching, mentoring, or coaching.

—Bobby Bogard, Executive Director, Linked
International Network of Churches (LINC)

Shannon has hit a grand-slam homerun out of the park with this book. I've known Shannon for many years, and he lives the principles he lays out for us in this book. A gift for godly marriages and those looking to make it better. This book is biblical, practical, and perfect for today. Whether you're single and contemplating marriage or you've been married for 50 years, this book will add value and vision for a great marriage. You'll be glad you read it.

—Dr. Chris Stephens, Senior Pastor
Faith Promise Church

Pastor Shannon has written a must-read for anyone remotely considering or currently engaged in marriage and parenting. Read this book, and learn from one of the best.

— Joel Cauley, Lead Pastor, Relevant Church

Shannon's years of married life and parenting come to life in *40,000 Words About Marriage & Parenting*. I highly recommend this book to anyone who is married or planning on being married someday.

—Luke Barnett, Senior Pastor Dream City Church, Phoenix, AZ

I'm grateful for Shannon O'Dell & the gift this book is to the church. He is so honest & forthright that his message will connect with anyone who's married or plans to be. His delivery has just enough humor that it makes for an easy read, even with a challenging topic.

—Mel Massengale, Lead Pastor, The Summit Church, Indiana, PA

Shannon's years of married life and parenting come to life in *40,000 Words About Marriage & Parenting*. I highly recommend this book to anyone who is married or planning on being married someday.

—Luke Barnett, Senior Pastor, Dream City Church Phoenix, AZ

Thank you, Shannon (and Cindy), for the wisdom found throughout this book! This is something my wife and I will come back to often.

Whether your family dynamics are in need of an overhaul or you just need to keep the romance with your spouse red hot, *40,000 Words About Marriage & Parenting* is a must-read!

—Andy Chrisman
Worship Pastor, Church on the Move / 4HIM

*40,000 Words About Marriage & Parenting* is a helpful guide full of practical tools for those who desire to build and enjoy the highest level of marital companionship. In addition to his pragmatic relationship guidance, Shannon addresses the power of parenting with intentionality to raise kids who will influence the culture in which they live. For over twenty years, Shannon has become a leading voice in helping to transform family lives nationwide, and I know this book will be an instrumental tool in building families all over the globe.

—Galen Woodward
Over Site Pastor at Citizen Church, Albuquerque, NM

Shannon is one of the most genius thinkers and creative communicators and has put that innovation into *40,000 Words* that will help define your marriage and parenting biblically. There is no greater need for our American culture than to understand the Creator's intent for marriage and His parenting design. Thank you, Shannon and Cindy, for creating a textbook that is simple and applicable to our homes.

—Marty Sloan
Senior Pastor, Calvary Church Naperville, IL

My friend Shannon has given you 40,000 Words to help improve your marriage and parenting, and overall home atmosphere. Honesty, creativity, and 29 years of experience are found on every page of the book and his partnering study guide.

—Brad Lomenick, Founder, BLINC
Author, *H3 Leadership* and *The Catalyst Leader*

# 40,000 WORDS

GOD'S HEART FOR YOUR HOME

*about*

# MARRIAGE & PARENTING

## SHANNON O'DELL

FO
UR

# OTHER BOOKS BY SHANNON O'DELL

*Transforming Church in Rural America:*
*Breaking All the Rurals*

*This book is possible because of two people…*
*My Bridegroom Jesus Christ*
*my Lord and Savior.*
*My beautiful bride Cindy O'Dell.*
*Teaching and writing about the institution*
*that God Almighty created to reflect His love*
*for humanity is so humbling.  It comes with*
*a mantle only given with anointing and*
*obedience to follow His map for marriage.*
*Thank you Cindy for giving the authority*
*to my life that made this possible.*
*Thank you Jesus for giving us*
*the only authoritative directive*
*and design for marriage.*

# Contents

*Acknowledgments* ........................................ xi
*Foreword* ................................................ xiii

Introduction: **Reflecting the Heart of God
to a Broken World** ....................................... 15

CHAPTER 1. **The Heart of Marriage** ........................ 21
      Chamber I: Love

CHAPTER 2. **The Heart of Marriage** ........................ 41
      Chamber II: Forgiveness

CHAPTER 3. **The Heart of Marriage** ........................ 63
      Chamber III: Communication

CHAPTER 4. **The Heart of Marriage** ........................ 87
      Chamber IV: Red-Hot Sex

CHAPTER 5. **The Heart of Parenting** ...................... 109
      Chamber I: Love

CHAPTER 6. **The Heart of Parenting** ...................... 131
      Chamber II: Honor

CHAPTER 7. **The Heart of Parenting** ...................... 155
      Chamber III: Training

CHAPTER 8. **The Heart of Parenting** ...................... 177
      Chamber IV: Truth

Afterward: **The Heart of the Gospel** ..................... 197

Going Further: **Romance Uncensored** ...................... 201
*About the Author.* ........................................ 203
*Appendix A: A Marriage Creed.* ............................ 205

# ACKNOWLEDGMENTS

This book is possible because of two people: My bridegroom, Jesus Christ, my Lord and Savior, and my beautiful bride, Cindy O'Dell.

Teaching and writing about the institution that God Almighty created to reflect His love for humanity is so humbling. It comes with a mantle only given with anointing and obedience to following His map for marriage.

Thank you, Cindy, for giving the authority to my life that made this possible. Thank you, Jesus, for giving us the only authoritative directive and design for marriage.

To my kids—thank you, Anna, Evan, Sara, and K.J., for leading lives that bring honor to God, and to your mother and me.

To my church—thank you, Brand New Church, for making it so much fun to serve God. Thank you, volunteers, leaders, and staff who allow me the privilege of writing and teaching Romance Uncensored around the country.

To my mentors—thank you, Pastor Ed Young Jr., for sparking creativity in my heart, and Pastor Willie George, for shaping my life, motivating my ministry call, and picking me up when I make mistakes.

To Gayle O'Dell—thank you, Mom, for explaining what the rapture was about (from your postcard on the family cork board) and sharing with me who Jesus was, sitting at our kitchen bar.

# FOREWORD

**M**y friend Shannon O'Dell has come up with a great addition to your marriage and family toolkit. These words will help you to adjust and repair—the most essential elements in any strong relationship.

I love people who are honest, the kind who acknowledge points of stress and deal with them until they're fixed. I've seen this at work in Shannon's family firsthand. This is not a theory—it's firsthand experience.

Make an investment of your time into these 40,000 words now that you've invested your money. I am certain that it will return a profit in the relationships that matter most.

Willie George
Founding Pastor
Church on the Move
Tulsa, Oklahoma

# REFLECTING THE HEART OF GOD TO A BROKEN WORLD

*Love each other with genuine affection, and
take delight in honoring each other.*
—ROMANS 12:10 (NLT)

S ome say that Jesus is coming back any day now; you can tell by looking at the terrible state of the world. Maybe. All I know for sure is that we're two thousand years closer to His return. And that I want as many people as possible to be part of His amazing new kingdom when He arrives.

In 30 years of preaching the gospel, I have used all kinds of metaphors and illustrations to tell people about God's amazing love for them. But I'm more and more convinced that the best picture the church has been given to share the good news isn't some parallel from the latest Hollywood blockbuster.

It's much more every day. It's the home. Marriage and family lived out as God always intended. Think about it. When God created humankind in His image, He made us male and female, the two coming together as one and creating the first family. The Bible speaks of Jesus as the bridegroom and the church as His bride. If you want to get a sense of God's love for the world, you should be able to see it in marriage.

But you've only got to look at the headlines to get a sense that something is deeply wrong. So many broken marriages. So much abandonment, abuse, addiction, and violence. So much confusion about sexual identity. There's a whole lot of crazy out there. But however bizarre some of it is, I don't find myself laughing. Nah. Actually, it all breaks my heart.

And yet. Things may be bad in our society right now, but I am kind of encouraged, in a way because people are desperate for answers. They are looking for love . . . just in all the wrong places.

However, even the smallest match can make a difference when it's really dark. And think about what happens when you strike a whole bunch of matches simultaneously, how much brighter it becomes.

That's the potential for the church in these days. God's heart for humankind beats in and through marriage and the family. Passion, protection, provision, purpose—they're all there to be seen in a godly home. What might happen if we were to better reflect to the world around us what marriage and parenting are really supposed to look like?

## BRAGGING ON MY GIRLFRIEND

When I work out at the gym and get chatting with some of the other guys there, I'll talk about my girlfriend (that's how she's identified on my phone) and how crazy I am about her. I don't explain right away that, actually, Cindy and I have been married coming up on thirty years. (Nor do I mention that I'm a pastor until they ask at some stage.) I talk about how great Cindy's and my relationship is, without getting locker-room inappropriate. They're often kind of intrigued and want to know more, so I'll invite them along to church. Over the years I have baptized around forty guys who have come to know Jesus through this process.

People are hungry for help in learning how to express and experience genuine, intimate love. So, why do so many churches seem to spend more time preaching about the end times than they do about marriage and parenting?

Sadly, because it's safer. It's easier to talk about the seven churches of Revelation and Jesus's return because that's all out there in the future, somewhere. Talk about marriage and parenting, and you are getting a little too close to home, literally.

I do not mean to sound critical, but some preachers don't want to talk about marriage because their wife is sitting in the front row, and they both know things aren't good between them. Or they avoid addressing parenting issues because their own kids are so lost.

I'm not saying we need to be perfect. Or pretend that we are—people can see through that in a heartbeat. Part of being a great witness to the world is to show how we deal with our failures in relationships. How we get back up when we fall. How we refuse to quit.

Biblical marriage and parenting are simply two of the best resources we have for sharing God's heart for the world with those who don't know Him.

It's not just about building a godly home so others get to learn about Jesus. It's about getting a taste of heaven on earth ourselves. Other than knowing Christ, being a husband and a father have been the two greatest experiences of my life. But it hasn't all been hearts and flowers. It hasn't always been easy (for them more than for me!). Sometimes it's required hard work. But you know what? Good things come at a price.

Sadly, too many people spend more time and money and effort on planning their wedding than they do preparing for or tending to their marriage. Then they spend a whole lot more money on attorneys and therapists.

I believe that both marriage and parenting reveal the heart of God to a world desperate to know real and lasting love. And just as a healthy heart has four chambers that need to beat in harmony for a body to function at its best, so both marriage and parenting have four essential parts.

Let's look at them together.

# CHAPTER ONE
# THE HEART OF MARRIAGE

## Chamber I: Love

*"As the Father has loved me, so have I loved you. Now remain
in my love . . . I have told you this so that my joy may be
in you and that your joy may be complete. My command is
this: Love each other as I have loved you. Greater love has
no one than this: to lay down one's life for one's friend."*
—JOHN 15:9, 11-13

To the uninformed people sitting in the booths around us, I must have looked like a giddy, babbling, twenty-year-old punk kid because, well, I guess I was a giddy, babbling, twenty-year-old punk kid.

I was in an Olive Garden in South Bend, Indiana. Cindy was sitting across from me on our first date: I felt suspended in bliss as the earth temporarily stopped rotating and every star in the universe twinkled in approval. My heart was overflowing with optimism, passion, and certainty—I knew that this was just the beginning. Man, I was in *love*.

But hold on a sec. Just what does that really mean? What actually is love? Let's ask the apostle Paul. After all, the Holy Spirit moved through him to write the Bible passage that is probably quoted in more weddings than any other!

> *Love never gives up.*
> *Love cares more for others than for self.*
> *Love doesn't want what it doesn't have.*
> *Love doesn't strut,*
> *Doesn't have a swelled head,*
> *Doesn't force itself on others,*
> *Isn't always "me first,"*
> *Doesn't fly off the handle,*
> *Doesn't keep score of the sins of others,*
> *Doesn't revel when others grovel,*
> *Takes pleasure in the flowering of truth,*
> *Puts up with anything,*
> *Trusts God always,*
> *Always looks for the best,*

*Never looks back,*
*But keeps going to the end.* —1 CORINTHIANS 13:4-7 (MSG)

Words like that sound like music in the ears of all giddy punks sitting in Olive Gardens everywhere. But fast forward a couple of years, when you are plunked down together at the dining room table. Forget the candles and the music. The everyday food seems bland—and then mix in some credit card debt, season it with some dirty diapers, and let it sit for a while in the middle of a lukewarm sexual relationship. The everyday reality of marriage can expose our bitter side like nothing else. Impatience, envy, pride, anger—marriage boils all that stuff to the surface.

Yes, sometimes the love that flowed so easily in the beginning gets blocked. We hit a wall. But *we stayed married because we love God, not because we feel in love.* Remember this when it feels like, blam!, you have hit a concrete barrier and parts are flying everywhere: There is evil in this world, spiritual and physical forces that want to keep you from dying with Christ and serving His love to your spouse.

Satan is a liar. He comes to steal, kill, and destroy (John 10:10), and it's been that way from the beginning. Note that he didn't turn up in the Garden of Eden to try to spoil God's creation until there was marriage. And what did he do then? Drive a wedge between the man and the woman. They covered themselves

up—hid from each other—and next thing you know, that bro-
kenness was to be seen in their kids' lives, with Cain killing Abel.

Here are four of the most common blockages he tries to use
to attack our marriages:

### Blockage Number 1: "If this thing doesn't work for me, I'm out of here."

Satan would like us to think that we can just back away from
marriage and slip out the back door, no harm, no foul. But
marriage is not a contract that can be broken anytime you feel
things are not going your way. Marriage is a covenant with
God, and He wants you to stay in it so that you can experience true joy. You stay married not because you feel in love but
because you love God. In a world that is increasingly all about
"me, me, me" and "finding yourself," that's revolutionary. God's
idea of marriage is not what you can get but what you can give.

Remember: When you smash into the wall of hopelessness,
the love of Christ in you can bust through!

### Blockage Number 2: "Women are from Venus and men are from Mars."

Hello? Of course men and women are different! Sheesh, just
look at the different ways our bodies are designed and then go

from there. God *made* men and women different. That's part of the plan. It's not an excuse to drift away and live in your own corners of the universe. God designed you to live together, with all your differences, right here on the same planet. If you are willing, you can discover this unity.

Remember: When you impact the wall of differences, the love of Christ in you can bust through!

## Blockage Number 3: *The Headache.*

You've maybe heard the line, "Not tonight, honey, I have a headache." Well, here's the plan, guys: Bring two aspirins and a glass of water into the bedroom and hand them to her. She will say, "What are these for? I don't have a headache." Then you say, "Sweet! Then let's get some candles and light it up!"

Seriously, if you're cutting your spouse off from sex on a regular basis (and this can be men; it goes both ways), you're cutting away little pieces of their heart every time. And it's not just about sex. We say "Not now, honey" in lots of different ways, and each time it communicates rejection.

"Not now, honey, I am busy coaching ... I have to work late ... I have a church meeting ... I have to fold the laundry ... I'm watching my show ..." How many hours do we waste zoning out in front of worthless junk on the tube with the remote, *click, click, click*? Maybe it's time to shut the stupid thing off and figure out what makes our spouse "click"?

The two of you were created to be intimate emotionally, spiritually, and physically. Are you shaming your spouse by saying "No"? Bear in mind that when you continually say "no" to intimacy, you are refusing fellowship with God because intimacy with your spouse is a form of worship to God.

Remember: When your marriage is constantly running into a wall of "headaches," the love of Christ in you can break through.

### Blockage Number 4: K.I.D.S. (Keeping Intimacy Distanced Successfully)

I'm all for awesome parenting: we'll get into all that a little later. Kids are near the top of God's priority list, but your spouse comes above them. If you let your kids dominate your marriage, everyone is likely to crash and burn. And it's not just kids. Your work, hobbies, and church life must come after your commitment to spending quality time with each other. You need time and space for the two of you.

Too many couples make the mistake of focusing all their attention on their kids. Then, when the last one grows up and leaves home, they don't really know each other anymore. Sadly, for a lot of couples, the empty nest means *emptiness*.

Remember: When you hit the wall of kids, all you may *really* need is a half-decent babysitter.

With all those distractions and diversions, is it any wonder the flame of marriage can grow dim? Pretty soon, Paul's definition of love seems not only impractical but maybe even impossible. However, that passage should sound familiar. Like this:

> *"My command is this: Love each other as I have loved you. Greater love has no one than this: to lay down one's life for one's friends ... You did not choose me, but I chose you and appointed you so that you might go and bear fruit—fruit that will last—and so that whatever you ask in my name the Father will give you. This is my command: Love each other."* —JOHN 15:12-13,16-17

Be honest with me now. You might read that and think, Yeah, right! I'm supposed to love like Jesus? Impossible. And you know what? You are right.

This kind of love is impossible if (like most people) you are trying to love out of your own strength and your own emotions.

Please, I ask you to hit the brakes right now and stop and think for a moment. If you get this next passage of Scripture, you'll get the key to love, the most important foundation in any relationship. But if you miss it, you might as well throw in the towel and call it quits. If you want to experience the kind of love Jesus talked about in John 15, you have got to go back and ponder what he said in the previous chapter:

*"If you love me, keep my commands. And I will ask the Father, and he will give you another advocate to help you and be with you forever— the Spirit of truth . . . for he lives with you and will be in you. I will not leave you as orphans; I will come to you . . . Whoever has my commands and keeps them is the one who loves me. The one who loves me will be loved by my Father, and I too will love them and show myself to them." Then Judas (not Judas Iscariot) said, "But, Lord, why do you intend to show yourself to us and not to the world?" Jesus replied, "Anyone who loves me will obey my teaching. My Father will love them, and we will come to them and make our home with them . . . I am the true vine, and my Father is the gardener. Remain in me, as I also remain in you. No branch can bear fruit by itself; it must remain in the vine. Neither can you bear fruit unless you remain in me. I am the vine; you are the branches. If you remain in me and I in you, you will bear much fruit; apart from me you can do nothing. This is to my Father's glory, that you bear much fruit, showing yourselves to be my disciples. As the Father has loved me, so have I loved you. Now remain in my love. If you keep my commands, you will remain in my love, just as I have kept my Father's commands and remain in his love. I have*

*told you this so that my joy may be in you and that your joy may be complete."* —JOHN 14:15-17, 21-23; 15:1, 4-5, 8-11

There's a tremendous amount of meat in this passage. Let's cut it up into the most important bite-sized chunks:

- Love is more important than anything else. It is the all-encompassing, universal command of God.
- We are commanded to love like Jesus loved us (sacrificing our lives for others).
- Without Christ, you can't do *anything* of real value (particularly something as difficult as loving others like Christ loves you).
- The Holy Spirit is with you and lives in you to help you (if you have opened the door of your life to Christ).
- By "remaining" in Christ's love you will "bear much fruit."

If you feel it's impossible to love your spouse right now, I get that. But that's because you're trying to love in your own strength rather than letting Christ love through you with His love.

*For Christ's love compels us, because we are convinced that one died for all, and therefore all died. And he died for all, that those who live should no longer live for themselves but for him who died for them and was raised again . . . Therefore, if anyone is in Christ, the new creation has come: The old has gone, the new is here! All this is*

> *from God, who reconciled us to himself through Christ
> and gave us the ministry of reconciliation.* —2 CORIN-
> THIANS 5: 14-15, 17-18

> *I can do all this through him who gives me strength.*
> —PHILIPPIANS 4:13

Let me share with you what I want for my life: When people come to me for help, I want to be so full of God's love that they can dip into my life and drink deeply from the Spirit and walk away changed in every way. So, I must stay full of God at all times; without Him, I have nothing to offer. And without Him, you have nothing to offer your spouse. He's the source of it all! You have to tap into that source—or you have nothing to offer.

> *Dear friends, let us love one another, for love comes from
> God. Everyone who loves has been born of God and knows
> God. Whoever does not love does not know God, because
> God is love. This is how God showed his love among us:
> He sent his one and only Son into the world that we might
> live through him.* —1 JOHN 4:7-9

It is *God's* love flowing through me that makes me the best husband to Cindy that I can be. And I'm telling you, it's the coolest thing possible: Cindy and I are one in Christ and, together with God we are strong. And it started when we committed to morning Bible reading, prayer together every night, and an open line of transparent communication. These three things have made all the difference.

Two years after that Olive Garden moment with Cindy, I knew it was time for me to ask her the most important question of my life.

She was more than eight hours away on a ministry project in Little Rock, Arkansas. In a couple of phone calls, I got everything scripted with the host family at the home where she and her team were staying. When she came in that night, they said, "Hey, we're going to go ahead and go to bed. Do you mind shutting off the light in the kitchen for us?" But when she walked in, she saw a Bible next to a candle on a small table in the center of the room—a Bible with my name on it. I heard her take a breath, and she started looking around. I came out of a back room where I had been hiding, and—let me tell you—I can still remember the way she felt when I held her in my arms. The way her hair laid on her shoulders, the smell of her perfume, everything.

Then I knelt by the table in front of her, looked into her eyes, and asked, "Would you spend the rest of your life with me?" We started bawling as I tried to get the box containing the $49 ring I had bought out of my pocket. (Okay, so I had gained a couple of extra pounds in the months we'd been apart and didn't have the chance to buy a bigger pair of pants.) I put that ring on her finger and kissed her for the first time. As our tears mixed with the warmth of that kiss, I read to her a passage of Scripture that God had given me:

> *You husbands in the same way, live with your wives in an understanding way, as with someone weaker, since she is a woman; and show her honor as a fellow heir of the grace of life, so that your prayers will not be hindered. To sum up, all of you be harmonious, sympathetic, brotherly, kindhearted, and humble in spirit; not returning evil for evil or insult for insult, but giving a blessing instead; for you were called for the very purpose that you might inherit a blessing.* —1 PETER 3:7-9 (NASB)

I wish I could say I've always obeyed it. But I haven't. There's been evil and insults, and there have been times that I have deeply wounded Cindy rather than showing her honor. If not for forgiveness, I don't know where we would be. But I've never forgotten that passage or the night I proposed. It was a major step. So let me suggest something to you right now. Why don't you step out and make a decision to serve up some love and honor to your spouse?

## REFLECTING THE LOVE OF CHRIST TO YOUR SPOUSE

Men, let me start with you. Marriage, like a dance, involves two people, but someone needs to lead. And I think it's no accident that the word *romance* has "man" in the middle. Guys, we're called to honor our wives and treat them with understanding "as with someone weaker." But get this right: Weaker doesn't mean less significant. We're talking about the difference between is the difference between steel and gold, clay and porcelain, denim and silk. Most importantly, she is a "fellow heir of the grace of life." Gentlemen, that means that she is a daughter of the King of kings and the Lord of lords, and she should be treated that way.

## HERE ARE SOME IDEAS TO GET YOU STARTED.

### Ten Ways a Man can Honor a Woman

*Prioritize Christ.* How does that happen? Through prayer, pondering the Bible, and listening to what Christ is telling you to do. Your relationship with Christ is the source and the foundation of all your other relationships. Make Him number one.

*Lead in shaping your kids.* Have a unified vision in discipline, direction, and devotion to Jesus Christ.

*Lead spiritually.* I know that is scary, and I know you might feel inadequate. But it's worth it, and Christ in you can help you do it. We'll talk more about how in the rest of the book.

*Defend her.* Guard her physically, emotionally, socially, and spiritually. You are the man. Protect and defend her, particularly where she is weaker.

*Give her the passwords!* Separate accounts breed separate lives. Give her access. Let her in. That's bank accounts, social media, mobile devices, and e-mail. There might be some damaging stuff in there, but if so, it's time to be honest and transparent.

*Serve her.* Think about where you can make her feel special and pampered and do it. Maybe pick the thing that she hates to have to do, man up, and do it yourself.

*Tell her.* You'll get more about this in the pages about communication, but for now find a unique way to tell her about just one thing that you like and love about her.

*Say "yes" and mean it.* You said "yes" at the altar. That meant forsaking all others. Keep it that way. Turn your back on the door. Burn your bridges and remove the girl at work from your Facebook friends list.

*Touch her.* Do it in front of your kids. Kiss her on the mouth and hug her when you head out the door in the morning, not just when you hope to get lucky at night. The kids may go "Eeuuw," but, secretly, they will love it.

*Date her.* She is still your girlfriend, so plan a great table date and make it a weekly habit.

Okay, ladies, it's your turn. If you want to know how to honor a man, be feminine-strong. Proverbs 14:1 says, "The wise woman builds her house, but with her own hands the foolish one tears her down." That's strong stuff, and the Scriptures are full of examples of women who showed this kind of strength.

Study women like Deborah. She was God-fearing; she recognized the leadership in her home. She led and was unbelievable. Deborah is the one that went into the tent and drove a tent peg into an enemy guy's head. Esther saved a whole nation because she was willing to face death for what was right. If you want some bullet points about how to honor a man through feminine strength, look at Proverbs 31.

### Ten Ways a Woman can Honor a Man

*Be full of faith.* It's your relationship with God that will be your strength. Keep God number one in your life so that He can live through you to love others as He loves you.

*Be trustworthy.* Say it and do it. It's that simple.

*Make marriage a priority.* Put your man on your to-do list. Commit to making your relationship better. Be willing to let

Christ love your husband through you. You may have to take the first move on this if your husband isn't ready to come to the table yet.

*Be serious about your time.* Manage your time well so that your highest priorities are at the top of the endless list of things that you need to get done, and the insignificant stuff that saps your energy and time doesn't get in the way.

*Be aware of your finances.* Don't go into neutral. Yes, there could be a situation where your husband is in charge ultimately of the overall financial situation of the home, but do what you can to assist him and know what's going on. Encourage him and affirm him when money is tight. It's hard on a guy, and he could really use your support.

*Be serious about mothering.* Those kids will be your family's legacy, and your family's legacy will honor your husband.

*Serve big-time.* I love going into a home where the wife is serious about serving the husband. Do you want to see a picture of God's church illuminated like never before? Be that wife. It's a beautiful, beautiful picture.

*Have an entrepreneurial spirit.* You can initiate things and create things that wouldn't exist without you. Never hesitate to step out in new ways in your marriage.

*Be a giver.* Nothing will crush your marriage faster than greed. The Lord will supply all your needs. You can give the best of what you have, what you can do, and who you are to your husband.

*Burn the "Honey-not-tonight" gown.* And while you're at it, torch the "granny panties." When you dress down for the night, dress it up for him. That will honor him in ways you probably can't even imagine.

Cindy and I have learned a lot about honoring each other over the last three decades. Most of it didn't come naturally, and a lot we never would've thought about on our own. But the flame still burns bright for us, and candles still flicker all the time because it comes from a deep bed of coals of glowing love; it's the love of God heating it all up.

Marriage is not a moment of passion. It's a momentous covenant call of God. You have to be reminded of that calling because, just like your walk with Christ, it's going to be ebb and flow, up and down, heaven and hell, drought and downpour. If it's rough and you are ready to bail, I get that. If it's just tough, and you're feeling really drained at the marriage table, I get that too. Maybe your marriage is doing okay, but you're ready to make the move from "good to great," or "great to awesome."

No matter where you are in your marriage, remember what Jesus did at the very beginning of His ministry—at a wedding. When they ran out of supplies, naturally it looked like the party was over. But Jesus did something supernatural: He went to the table, took ordinary, bland water and turned it into wine—but not just *any* wine, it was *fine* wine, the *best* wine that they had been served that night.

Maybe you are in need of a miracle too. Believe it or not, Jesus in you can do the impossible. Just remember, the first miracle of Jesus happened at a wedding. Maybe you want to join me in this prayer:

> *Lord Jesus,*
> *Thank you for coming into my life. Thank you for putting your Holy Spirit in me so I can know your love and so You can love others through me. I agree with Your scriptures that say I can do nothing apart from You. So, I ask You to show me how You want me to honor and bless my spouse and all people around me. Fill me with hope, give me the willingness to obey, for I believe that You are the God of love and miracles.*
> *Amen.*

## A HEART CHECKUP: LOVE

- Find somewhere you can experience the presence of Christ and His Holy Spirit without distraction or interruption. I believe He has a lot to tell you through His Word and through His Spirit.

- Ponder John 14-15. Really think about God's love for you. John wrote that "we love because he first loved us." Ask God to make these passages come alive to you so that God's love for you is etched firmly in your heart.
- Pray with honesty. I mean, really pour your heart out about where you are in your marriage.
- Ponder 1 Peter 3. There's a lot of deep stuff here. Let it soak in.
- Listen to His lead. Through the Bible and through His Spirit, I believe God will give you direction and hope, and even show you the specific ways that He wants you to honor and bless your spouse.
- Share your heartbeat. Carve out a special time with your spouse. Why don't you pick one of their favorite places to go? But give it some thought ahead of time. Pray through the list of ten ways you can honor your spouse. Seriously consider the different ways that you can bless them when you're together. Be willing to follow Christ's lead no matter how crazy or uncomfortable it might seem. You're charting new ground here. You may not do it perfectly, and it might be awkward. Your spouse might not even receive it, but go for it! You're serving the love of Christ to your spouse.

## CHAPTER TWO
# THE HEART OF MARRIAGE

## Chamber II: Forgiveness

*God made you alive with Christ. He forgave us
all our sins, having canceled the charge of our legal
indebtedness, which stood against us and condemned
us; he has taken it away, nailing it to the cross.*
—COLOSSIANS 2:13-14

I am not Jesus. (Now there's a revelation! Aren't you glad you bought this book?) But sometimes, people think a pastor should be more like Jesus than other mere mortals. The fact is, we are just dudes with all the doubts, struggles, and temptations of a regular Joe. And one night early in our marriage, that was graphically obvious.

I had a youth pastor gig. Great job. I loved it. But one of the young women in our group was shopping for love in all the wrong places, and she was selling everything she had to get it. I wish I could be more spiritual about it, but I'm just telling it like it was.

We had the no PDA (public display of affection) rule in our group, but we did allow the "Christian side-hug." That night she gave me the side-hug, and I side-hugged her back—ministry stuff, right? I'm affirming this gal, just letting her know her value before God, encouraging her in her walk with Christ . . . and then, the twist. We pivoted in a way that pressed her chest to mine. It lasted only a second or two, but it felt like minutes—and in all honesty, at that moment, every molecule of my flesh wished it could last for hours. I allowed myself to be carried away by lust, and the lust gave birth to full-blown sin in my mind, just as the Bible says it will (James 1:15).

It took a little while to shake it off. Later that night, I confessed it to God, and vowed to keep my distance from her and move on. *Praise the Lord. No harm done. Nobody knows. Nobody needs to know. Just forget it.*

Fast forward a few months. I was officiating a revival meeting, of all things, a big spiritual mountaintop type of deal. I was sitting next to Cindy, thinking about how I was going to close the meeting. "Thanks for being here! Wow, didn't God speak to us tonight? Hallelujah, glory to God. Amen, brother! Hallelujah! *Somebody say amen!*" Yeah, that would wrap it up, we would take an offering, and everybody would think I was awesome.

But then I heard it, that quiet voice that sometimes shouts in our souls. *Shannon, remember that girl? You have to tell Cindy right now that you lusted.*

"Thanks, God, but I need to close this service," I prayed. "I will get on that later, okay?"

I tried to refocus on what was happening around me and prepare for what I was going to do, but the dodge didn't work. It's a little hard to fake God out. The voice of the Spirit wouldn't shut up, and this time, God's conviction hit full force. Feelings of guilt rushed through my veins. I didn't want to tell Cindy at all, of course, but now? When I'm leading a revival? This was out of the question.

"Lord, you want me to tell my wife that I had sex in my mind with a teenage girl? Now?"

*Shannon, you need to clear your conscience. If you can't share and clear your conscience here with your earthly bride, then how are you going to be able to walk with your groom Jesus?*

Seriously, it felt like everything in the room froze. The speaker was still speaking, but I couldn't hear it. People were all around, but it was like I couldn't see them. Everything inside of me wanted to deny and ignore it. There was just too much at stake. We had only been married three years. This could crush her. I could see her running from the room. I could see myself hitchhiking home and finding my stuff scattered all over the front lawn.

I could feel myself beginning to shake inside and sweat on the outside.

*God, I can't tell her that. She's gonna leave me. I, I just can't, not right now.*

And I was partly right. *I* couldn't do it. But Christ in me could if I let Him. And my stalling techniques weren't working anyway. I knew better than that: Delayed obedience is disobedience. So, I took a deep breath, and the words started to flow from my mouth.

"Babe, I need to talk to you about something."

"Sure. Okay," she said, waiting.

"No," I said. "We need to get on our knees, and you need to put your hands behind your back." We knelt right there in the front row.

"Cindy, I lusted in my heart for another woman . . ." I told her the whole situation. She was quiet for a few seconds (which is rarely good), but I knew at that moment the timing was right. The Spirit of God had told me to do exactly what I did. Now it was out of my control.

Cindy looked over at me and put her arm around my shoulders and pulled me close; I can still almost even smell her sweet breath on my cheek.

She looked at me and said, "Babe, I love you more right now than I have ever loved you."

I started to cry. When I looked at her, I *saw* Cindy, but then a powerful realization rushed over me. I was *looking* at Jesus. It was Jesus in her, forgiving me through her, because one day, He was scourged, beaten until He was unrecognizable as a human. It was Jesus saying, "I love you more now than ever. I love you more now than ever." It was Jesus in her that willingly hung on the cross, bleeding there for me until He could barely breathe, finally gasping, "It is finished." *Tetelestai!* in the Greek. Paid in full. Cindy had taken my sin to the cross, where God crucified it with Christ.

And then, Christ rose again . . . and so did Cindy and I. We slowly stood up together, more powerful, more anointed, and more ready to do ministry than we ever had been before when I sat there and I lied to her in my silence. That transparency brought unbelievable relational beauty. Sin had died and intimacy lived.

Nothing would be the same after this. Cindy taught me that day that we do not stay married because we feel in love but because we love God.

## A LONG TIME AGO, IN A GARDEN FAR AWAY

After God finished creating the heavens and the earth and filling it with plants, animals, and the first man, He said it was "good." After He created Eve, however, and put her together with Adam, He called it "very good." Scripture says that the man and the woman were naked and they were not ashamed. (and I say, "Amen! Praise God for that.")

But just a few verses ahead, Adam and Eve rejected God's perfectly created order and disobeyed the boundaries that He had created for their protection. BLAM! Just like that, everything changed. Innocence was lost. Purity was defiled, and "they suddenly felt shame at their nakedness" (Genesis 3:7, NLT). The implications of this one act were cataclysmic. It was a

10.0 earthquake on the relationship scale. Unity with God was broken, and their relationship with each other quickly dissolved into a fearful game of blame. It was a natural consequence:

Whenever sin lives, intimacy dies.

We all struggle with intimacy issues with God and others. But you may be thinking, Shannon, I don't have any big sins. Really? You must realize that any sin is sin. Take pride, for instance. When you become prideful, intimacy dies. I know that many of you are asking, "Why is there no intimacy in our marriage? Where did it go? Why is he (or she) no longer pursuing me?" If sin is allowed to live, it will kill your relationship. Even secret sins that live only in your head will destroy intimacy with your spouse. When sin lives, intimacy dies not only with your spouse but also with God, your kids, your friends, your parents . . . everyone.

With so much sin living around us, in us, and between us, is it ever possible that we can be naked and unashamed again? The answer can be found in Jesus's encounter with a woman who had lived a sinful life. She learned that:

> *Jesus was eating at the Pharisee's house, so she came there with an alabaster jar of perfume. As she stood behind him at his feet weeping, she began to wet his feet with her tears. Then she wiped them with her hair, kissed them and poured*

*perfume on them. When the Pharisee who had invited him saw this, he said to himself, "If this man were a prophet, he would know who is touching him and what kind of woman she is—that she is a sinner."* —LUKE 7:37-39

Check this out: the Pharisee was saying this "to himself," but Jesus heard it loud and clear. And He answered with a story—one that should give hope to all of us who experience the broken intimacy caused by sin.

*Jesus answered him, "Simon, I have something to tell you." "Tell me, teacher," he said. "Two people owed money to a certain moneylender. One owed him five hundred denarii, and the other fifty. Neither of them had the money to pay him back, so he forgave the debts of both. Now which of them will love him more?" Simon replied, "I suppose the one who had the bigger debt forgiven." "You have judged correctly," Jesus said. Then he turned toward the woman and said to Simon, "Do you see this woman? I came into your house. You did not give me any water for my feet, but she wet my feet with her tears and wiped them with her hair. You did not give me a kiss, but this woman, from the time I entered, has not stopped kissing my feet. You did not put oil on my head, but she has poured perfume on my feet. Therefore, I tell you, her many sins have been forgiven—as her great love has shown. But whoever has been forgiven little loves little." Then Jesus said to her,*

*"Your sins are forgiven." The other guests began to say among themselves, "Who is this who even forgives sins?" Jesus said to the woman, "Your faith has saved you; go in peace."* —LUKE 7:40-50

I, for one, think that rocks. What happened that night set the stage for what was to play out on a cross outside Jerusalem shortly after this dinner. Jesus not only received a notorious sinner, but He knew what to do with her sin—and my sin, and yours.

*When you were dead in your sins and in the uncircumcision of your flesh, God made you alive with Christ. He forgave us all our sins, having canceled the charge of our legal indebtedness, which stood against us and condemned us; he has taken it away, nailing it to the cross.* —COLOSSIANS 2:13-14

This is one powerful word picture, and it's based on what really happened. God took your sins and He killed them. He nailed them to the cross with Jesus. Can you see it? Can you imagine your sins being pounded onto the rough wood beams where Jesus hung and died? Forgiveness is the divine transaction, paid in full by the blood of Jesus, which frees both the offender and the offended from the bondage of sin:

Whenever sin dies, intimacy lives!

But let me back up for a moment, because many of us have lived in denial and repression of our sin. Why? My guess is that most of us don't know how to handle our sin. And without forgiveness, it's just too much to handle, so we stuff it away somewhere in our souls. The first step in healing broken intimacy is sincerely recognizing what you have done. And it's not just what you have done; it's also what you have thought and said:

> *If we claim to be without sin, we deceive ourselves and the truth is not in us. If we confess our sins, he is faithful and just and will forgive us our sins and purify us from all unrighteousness.* —1 JOHN 1:8-9

When forgiveness flows, sin dies and intimacy flourishes. Forgiveness unleashes a freedom that sets the captives free.

## FINDING TRUE FORGIVENESS

The restoration of intimacy starts when you get real with God and let His forgiveness flow into your life first. Then that forgiveness can flow to others and start healing your relationships. The Bible shows the steps to get you there:

*Get transparent.* God knows everything. We might as well be honest. His Word and His Spirit in you will reveal specific sins that He wants to deal with. "Search me, God, and know my heart; test me and know my anxious thoughts. See if there is any offensive way in me, and lead me in the way everlasting" (Psalm 139:23-24).

*Agree.* When you accept as true what the Holy Spirit reveals about your sin, the Father forgives you, and the blood of Jesus cleanses you from guilt and shame. "If we confess our sins, he is faithful and just and will forgive us our sins and purify us from all unrighteousness" (1 John 1:9).

*Imagine.* Close your eyes and see God taking that list of your sins and nailing it to the cross where Jesus is hanging. "Having canceled the charge of our legal indebtedness, which stood against us and condemned us; he has taken it away, nailing it to the cross" (Colossians 2:14).

*Praise God!* Worship Him for what He has done and soak in the intimacy of your relationship with Him again. "Blessed is the one whose transgressions are forgiven, whose sins are covered" (Psalm 32:1).

## OFFERING TRUE FORGIVENESS

Several years ago, Cindy had an affair. She didn't do anything inappropriate—no sexual contact, and she never even met with the guy in private. It was an affair of the heart—an emotional connection with another man where she began to feed off his affection and attention. When the Spirit convicted her, she knew that she had crossed the line: this was emotional adultery. She came to me with that, and I'm telling you, it hit me hard, and it hurt me deeply.

I had a choice now. I could either wallow in that pain, letting it fester into bitterness, resentment, and anger, or I could release it to God, be free, and begin healing. It seems like an obvious choice. In all honesty, it's not an easy one to make. Pride is such a powerful thing, but thankfully the truth of God and the power of His Spirit in us is stronger.

> *Get rid of all bitterness, rage and anger, brawling and slander, along with every form of malice. Be kind and compassionate to one another, forgiving each other, just as in Christ God forgave you.* —EPHESIANS 4:31-32

Let me make something clear, though. Forgiveness does not mean forgetting. It doesn't mean that you return to an abusive situation. And it doesn't mean that there won't be natural consequences for the other person. Forgiveness frees *you* from the anger and bitterness caused by *their* actions. When you've been wounded, forgiveness is the only way to healing.

But how can you forgive others like Christ forgave you? You can't (just like you can't love like God loves), but Christ in you can. Here's how:

*Remember.* Get real with God. You'll need to "embrace the wrong" that has happened to you. Don't deny it or suppress it or make excuses for the one who has hurt you.

*Trust.* Recognize that true forgiveness only happens when you rely on Christ to forgive through you. You'll really need to activate your mind to do this. Forgiveness is a choice, not an emotion. "I can do all this through him who gives me strength" (Philippians 4:13).

*Release.* Pray, "Jesus, thank You for forgiving me. I let go of the pain that this has caused and will not hold it against them. You are just. I trust You to punish them if You say that is appropriate." "Do not take revenge, my dear friends, but leave room for God's wrath, for it is written: 'It is mine to avenge; I will repay,' says the Lord" (Romans 12:19).

*Bless.* Listen, I know this one sounds crazy at first, but the full healing power of forgiveness is unleashed when you turn around and do something that blesses the person who hurt you. When you do something right for someone who has wronged you, you shatter the division that Satan wants to see in relationships, and you take a major step towards the intimacy and healing that God designed.

> *Finally, all of you, be like-minded, be sympathetic, love one another, be compassionate and humble. Do not repay*

*evil with evil or insult with insult. On the contrary, repay*
*evil with blessing, because to this you were called so that*
*you may inherit a blessing.* —1 PETER 3:8-9

## SEEKING TRUE FORGIVENESS

It's one thing to be wounded; it's another to be the one who has caused the wound. The way to be free from the mental and emotional weight of your sin against someone else is to seek their forgiveness. I'm not saying this is easy. I am saying it's required. It's so important that Jesus said this process should even interrupt your normal worship routine:

> *Therefore, if you are offering your gift at the altar and*
> *there remember that your brother or sister has something*
> *against you, leave your gift there in front of the altar. First*
> *go and be reconciled to them; then come and offer your gift.*
> —MATTHEW 5:23-24

The process of asking for forgiveness is fairly simple, as you will see in a second (it's just not easy!). But let me advise you: If you need to ask for forgiveness for something seriously major that your spouse doesn't know about, I recommend talking with a pastor or a professional counselor beforehand. They will pray with you and help you put together a plan to bring what you have done to the table.

Cindy and I *regularly* go to a professional counselor to mediate our relationship. A lot of people have personal trainers or business consultants. Cindy and I know that our relationship is far more important than our bodies or bucks, so we find the best help we can. A pro will help you walk through it.

How to request forgiveness:

*Recognize.* Let God search your heart and show you your ways. And then see your sin for what it is. Own up to it. Be responsible for it.

*Thank.* Let God know that you deeply appreciate His forgiveness. Ultimately, all sin is against God, and His forgiveness cleanses you and frees you from the things you have done against others.

*Ask.* When the time comes, tell the person specifically what you know you did to wrong them. Tell them you are sorry that you did it. And then say the four hardest words to say: *Will you forgive me?*

*Be free.* Asking for forgiveness doesn't necessarily mean that you're going to get forgiveness. With God, forgiveness is guaranteed. With people, you never know. Sometimes it takes a while before people are willing to let Christ forgive through them. Sometimes it never happens. The person you hurt might even go to the grave holding on to the pain you caused. That's hard, but it's out of your hands. Either way, you should willingly accept the natural consequences of your actions and then move on, knowing that God nailed those sins to the cross.

> *Therefore, there is now no condemnation for those who are in Christ Jesus, because through Christ Jesus the law of the Spirit who gives life has set you free from the law of sin and death.* —ROMANS 8:1-2

How do you know when you have truly forgiven someone or when they have truly forgiven you? When you or they don't keep bringing whatever it was up when you next have conflict. It's dead and buried. There's nothing blocking that free flow of love.

Unfaithfulness cuts deep, I know. But wounding as it is, adultery is not the unforgivable sin (blasphemy against the Holy Spirit is: Matthew 12:31). If you have cheated or been cheated on, there's still hope. I've worked with couples who have experienced adultery and been able to renew and deepen their love for one another with God's help.

Cindy's emotional affair and my lust for a teenage girl could have been the end of our relationship—but forgiveness brought new life to us instead. Those two moments are among the most powerful we have ever experienced in our entire marriage. They were humbling, terrifying, and could have meant the death of our intimacy. But forgiveness flowed and it brought about some of the greatest beauty our marriage has ever experienced.

When sin dies at the cross of forgiveness, get ready for the resurrection in your marriage.

Forgiveness is always the new beginning of a deep intimacy. God forgives us completely and entirely; He died for sins once and for all. The process of experiencing and expressing His forgiveness in marriage never ends. This is a new way of life!

Thank God for His forgiveness; forgive others and seek forgiveness from others. Because when sin tries to kill your intimacy, you can put it to death on the cross, time after time after time, with forgiveness.

Perhaps you want to pray this with me:

> *My God,*
> *I believe that You are the God of forgiveness. By the power of your Holy Spirit in me, I ask that forgiveness would flow to me and through me. With all my heart, I am eternally thankful for Your forgiveness. Empower me to forgive others. Give me the courage to seek forgiveness from those I have sinned against. Together, let's nail all that sin to the cross and let it die, so that intimacy will live in my*

*relationship with You, my mate, and everyone you have*
*placed in my life.*
*Amen.*

## A HEART CHECKUP: FORGIVENESS

- Before you come aside for some focused time with Christ, do a simple arts and crafts project: Make a cross! Cardboard works fine, but you'll need some extra staples or pins. Two pieces of wood would work too, if you have a couple of extra nails. Seriously, do it! We are going to crucify some sin.

- All relationships need regular forgiveness to free them for intimacy. You'll want to go through the following steps for each important person in your life. But since this is the marriage section, start with your mate.

- Ponder. Spend some time soaking in Colossians 2. That chapter is filled with sin-slaughtering truth. Underline and circle the passages that the Holy Spirit emphasizes for you.

- Pray. Read the words of Psalm 139, but make this prayer of David your prayer. Go through it thought by thought, sharing your thoughts with God. Ask Him to show you how you have sinned against your spouse.

- Listen. Get transparent. Be honest with yourself and God as His Word and His Spirit reveal specific sins that He wants to deal with.

- Agree. Accept as true what the Holy Spirit reveals about your sin toward your spouse. Write them down!
- Imagine. Close your eyes and see God taking that list of your sins and nailing it to the cross where Jesus is hanging. Then actually do it. Nail your list of sins to the cross you made. Know that God really put those sins to death on the cross of Christ.
- Praise God! Worship Him for what He has done and soak in the intimacy of your relationship with Him. Forgiveness is awesome. Be free in what He has done for you!

Now, let's walk through it again, but this time you will release yourself from the sins your spouse has committed against you.

- Ponder. Spend some time thinking about Ephesians 4. Skim the whole chapter, marking it up as you go along. Pay close attention to verses 28-32.
- Pray. Ask the Holy Spirit to guide you and empower you to deal with the pain and hurt your mate has caused.
- Remember. Embrace the wrong that your spouse has done to you. Go ahead and make a list.
- Trust. You can forgive through Christ who gives you strength. Tell God you are depending on Him to make you willing and able.
- Release. Pray through each item. "Jesus, thank You for forgiving me. I let go of the pain that this has caused and will not hold it against them. You are just. I trust You to

punish them if You think it is appropriate." When you are all done, destroy this list! Unless your spouse specifically asks for your forgiveness for these things, you don't even need to tell them they are forgiven.

- Bless. You know the things that mean the most to your spouse. Ask God to help you pick one special way to bless them, then do it ASAP.

## EXPERIENCING FORGIVENESS TOGETHER

Ideally, the two of you are going through this book together. If so, set a date in a very private place. Be praying for your time together. You might want to fast for a period beforehand. Be sure you have some time alone with Christ before you come together. This is holy ground, the real deal. I know it sounds awkward and strange, but if you want to see resurrection in your marriage, the death of sin through radical forgiveness is how you do it.

When you come together, bring the crosses you both made and the list of sins that you have committed against your spouse.

- *Ponder.* Read Romans 8:1-12 together.
- *Pray.* Ask God to put sin to death in your marriage.
- *Recognize.* Take turns sharing your list of sins against each other. Make no excuses. Own up to it. Be responsible for it.

- *Thank.* Let them know that you believe God has forgiven you for your sin, and that you have thanked Him and praised Him for it.
- *Ask.* Tell them you are sorry for what you did. And then say the four hardest words to say: *Will you forgive me?*
- *Be free.* Take the list of sins your spouse has confessed to you and nail them to your cross. Then, together, praise God for taking all your sins to the cross and crucifying them. Destroy the lists together!

And one last thing. Back in the garden, before sin entered the equation, Adam and Eve were "naked and not ashamed." The blood of Jesus has wiped away our sin and shame. When the two of you embrace that forgiveness, sin dies, and intimacy is resurrected. Getting shamelessly naked together is a great way to celebrate. Just an idea ...

# CHAPTER THREE

# THE HEART OF MARRIAGE

## Chamber III: Communication

*And this is my prayer: that your love may abound more and more in knowledge and depth of insight, so that you may be able to discern what is best and may be pure and blameless for the day of Christ, filled with the fruit of righteousness that comes through Jesus Christ—to the glory and praise of God.*
—PHILIPPIANS 1:9-11

indy was frustrated. She was trying to tell me I wasn't listening to her—at least, I think that's what she said. (I wasn't really paying attention.) I saw her mouth moving, and the sound of her voice was bouncing around somewhere in my head, but it just wasn't connecting with my brain (so it sure wasn't connecting with my heart either).

I'm a pastor; I get paid to talk, not so much listen. I'm a professional *speaker* . . . But that doesn't mean I'm a good *communicator*. Talking comes easy. But when it comes to communication, I'm a piece of work, and I need to work at it. And you know what? It's worth it. Communication in marriage is not just a back-and-forth exchange of information and ideas. The *process* is an extension of the oneness that God created between a man and a woman way back in Eden:

> *"Then the LORD God made a woman from the rib he had taken out of the man, and he brought her to the man. The man said, 'This is now bone of my bones and flesh of my flesh; she shall be called "woman," for she was taken out of man.' That is why a man leaves his father and mother and is united to his wife, and they become one flesh."*
> —GENESIS 2:22-24

How many times have you "won" an argument with your spouse only to realize the both of you have lost? Why is that? It's because you're arguing with yourself, because the two of you are now one in Jesus. When you stiff-arm your spouse? You're stiff-arming yourself, because the two of you are one. When you criticize your spouse? Yep, you just do it to yourself. That's why it feels so awful afterward, even when you appear to have gotten the upper hand.

And some of the stuff we argue about? It's just crazy!

"You took my keys."

"No, I didn't."

"Yes, you did. I guarantee you had them last."

"No, I didn't!"

"Yes, you did! And then next thing you know, it's like Mount St. Helens blows up in your living room—and then you do find the car keys in your own pocket. (I hate it when that happens!)

Well, you might as well just drive on down to the attorney's office and get started on the divorce papers. Okay, maybe not exactly. You don't end up in divorce court over one incident like that. And you don't just decide one afternoon to jump in bed with the person working in the cubicle next to you. No, it's ten thousand itty-bitty steps that get you there. And every step of the way, there has been a breakdown in the way God designed communication to work to unify your marriage.

We all started off better than that. I remember one time I bought Cindy a cheap sweater at Walmart. Then I got some puffy paint and wrote her a love letter on the front of the shirt. I accidentally misspelled two of the words (really embarrassing), but I still did it because I wanted to communicate. Cindy rolled her eyes, but she loved it. One year, I wrote her a letter every day. We still have those letters. If things get tough, I can read them to myself and remind myself how much I love her.

Most relationships start out with that sort of stuff, but a few years go by, and then we find ourselves not communicating as effectively as we did back when we were dating. What has happened? Why did we stop being effective communicators?"

Here's why: Somewhere along the way, a subtle shift takes place. We start communicating not to become *one*, but to *win*. We try to negotiate. But if just one spouse wins, both lose—because God designed us to be one. Great communication isn't about getting our way; it's about doing it God's way.

Sometimes, you'll hear people talk about a win-win situation. That may work in business or politics, but it doesn't work in marriage. Because a win-win is based on compromise. The kind of oneness God intended for marriage isn't based on compromise but on agreement. "Can two people walk together without agreeing on the direction?" (Amos 3:3, NLT).

*And this is my prayer: that your love may abound more and more in knowledge and depth of insight, so that you may be able to discern what is best and may be pure and blameless for the day of Christ, filled with the fruit of righteousness that comes through Jesus Christ—to the glory and praise of God.* —PHILIPPIANS 1:9-11

What a powerful prayer! Who wouldn't want that kind of love in their marriage? Notice that love abounds "in knowledge and depth of insight"—a key phrase there. Knowledge and insight can come through awesome communication, so you can "discern what is best and may be pure."

The heart of marriage can't beat well without the healthy chambers of love and forgiveness. But it's this third chamber, communication, that makes the pulse strong and enduring, permanent, not likely to fall or give way.

## BRINGING CONFLICT TO A H.A.L.T.

The most important communication skill is as profound as it is simple. But it takes discernment, wisdom, and willingness to let the Spirit of God reveal it and then apply it. What is it? Shut up. That's it: Know when to close your trap, and you can derail the vast majority of destructive communication.

How do you know when to put a cork in it? Answering "Yes" to any one of the following four questions means it's time to H.A.L.T. the conversation:

**H**: "Am I hungry?" HALT!
**A**: "Am I angry?" HALT!
**L**: "Am I lonely?" HALT!
**T**: "Am I tired?" HALT!

## When You're Hungry

Trying to communicate when hungry can easily spark conflict. It can also lead to some really stupid decisions. Esau is a classic example. He came home from a day of hunting, and he was starving. Check out the dialog in Genesis 25. Seriously, he sounds a lot like me when I'm hungry. He was gruff, impatient, demanding, and extremely shortsighted. Because of his hunger, he entered into negotiations with his brother, Jacob, and actually gave up the inheritance of his birthright for a bowl of soup! If he would've recognized that he was hungry and that he needed to H.A.L.T. the conversation, he would've been a lot better off and would have broken the negotiation/conflict cycle immediately.

Here are a couple of magic phrases to consider when your stomach is rumbling:

"Honey, I'm famished. Let's talk about this after I've had some chow."

"I understand this is important. Can we talk about it while we eat?"

## When You're Angry

*Therefore each of you must put off falsehood and speak truthfully to your neighbor, for we are all members of one body. 'In your anger do not sin': Do not let the sun go down while you are still angry, and do not give the devil a foothold.*
—EPHESIANS 4:25-27

In our fallen world full of sin, anger is a part of life. It's possible to be angry and not sin, and forgiveness defuses anger before it has a chance to really explode. Anger needs to be dealt with. When Paul says, "Don't let the sun go down while you are still angry," I don't think he means that literally. If you get angry in the evening, you don't have to figure it out before sunset in five minutes. If you get ticked off just after dusk, that doesn't mean you have twenty-four hours to run around with steam pouring out of your ears. He's saying deal with it *soon*. You can be angry and not sin; but staying angry leads to an awful lot of sin. "Do not let your mouth lead you into sin" (Ecclesiastes 5:6). "An angry person stirs up conflict, and a hot-tempered person commits many sins" (Proverbs 29:22).

It's not unbiblical to argue with your mate as long as you are sincerely working toward oneness. In fact, I will go one step further and say, don't waste a good argument! Learn and grow from it. Anger, however, can launch you into the negotiation and conflict spiral, where all you ever do is argue. That's different. It may be because you're unwilling to relinquish your pride and truly come to a biblical resolution that creates a marital resolve. If neither one of you is willing to submit to God and each other, it's going to be a mess. So, when you realize you are angry, H.A.L.T., back off and shut up.

Some magic phrases:

"My attitude stinks right now, and it's getting worse. Give me a while to cool down."

"Let's take a break so I can take a deep breath. Can we sit down at the table tonight with a cup of coffee?"

"I can tell you are frustrated right now. Let's call a time out and come back to this later." (Just be sure you do.)

If this doesn't help you break the cycle, or if your anger *ever* reaches a point where there is the possibility of you becoming emotionally or physically abusive, get help before you hurt anyone further. Period.

**When You're Lonely**

It's really hard to communicate well when you feel disconnected. When negotiations fail and the conflict has worn you out, you might feel really alone. That is not a good time to try to talk *until* you take it to Christ and have some real heart-to-heart time with Him.

Hebrews 13:4-5 says: "Marriage should be honored by all, and the marriage bed kept pure, for God will judge the adulterer and all the sexually immoral. Keep your lives free from the love of money and be content with what you have because God has said, 'Never will I leave you; never will I forsake you.'" Do you see the connection? How many affairs might have been avoided, how many arguments about money could have been dodged, if we had just chosen to H.A.L.T. and spend some time restoring our connection with God, who has promised to never leave us or forsake us?

Loneliness is tough . . . it sucks the life out of you. When you're not experiencing oneness with your spouse, be sure you are finding it with your Lord. Then you can come back to your marriage with a full tank of love and start communicating in a way that leads toward oneness rather than negotiation and conflict.

Magic phrases:

"Hey, I'm kind of hurting right now. I'm going to spend some time with the Lord, and then maybe we can pick up this conversation after that."

"I can tell you're feeling alone, isolated, and unappreciated right now. Why don't we go get naked or go for a walk in the park (or whatever speaks love to your mate) and then pray about this?"

## When You're Tired

I don't need to explain this one, do I? You know what happens to you when you haven't had enough sleep. Recognize it and H.A.L.T. communication before you tip over into negotiation and conflict.

Magic phrases:

"Honey, I'm bushed. Let me sleep on it and we will talk about it over breakfast."

"I can tell you are worn out. No need to figure this out right now. I'll take care of the kids; you take a nap, and then we can talk about it."

Remember Paul's prayer "that your love may abound more and more in knowledge and depth of insight"? That only happens when somebody listens. Awesome communication becomes possible when you shut up. It *begins* when you listen—and I mean *really* listen. I'm not talking about nodding your head while formulating your next comeback as the other person talks. I'm talking about *active* listening that seeks knowledge and insight from the *other* person by asking good questions. Active listening:

*Buys* you time to get your head together and your heart in the right place.

*Helps* you understand what's going on so you can eventually respond in wisdom.

*Affirms* the other's importance by making them feel understood and loved.

*Leads* to good decisions.

Some magic phrases:

"I'm not sure I understand. Can you explain that in a different way?"

"So, what you are saying is___. Do I have it right?".

"Do you feel like I've heard you out?"

## MASTERING THE THREE TS

Having looked at some things not to do, now let's consider three essential keys to healthy communication: touch, tone, and timing. Let's look at each of them in turn.

### Reach Out and Touch

When couples come to me for help in their marriage, I can usually tell where things are at before either of them says a word. If they're sitting on the couch together rigidly, making sure their bodies don't touch, I know they are not in a good place relationally.

We all know how physical touch releases feel-good chemicals in our bodies. Holding hands while you're talking removes barriers. It softens you to each other and makes you more careful about the words you use. Let's just be clear, guys, that I'm talking here about nonsexual touch—touch that is about affirmation and appreciation, not arousal. Having said that, it will probably lead to greater intimacy in due course.

We need to respect each other's levels of comfort with physical touch. Cindy and I are plenty affectionate with each other, but I'm not much of a hand-holder when we're out in public. That's not because I don't love her; it's just that with my short legs and long arms, holding hands is kind of awkward. For some, physical touch is difficult because of unresolved issues from the past, maybe abuse. Here you may need some professional help to work through those things.

There are other ways to "touch your partner, too. Direct eye contact. A handwritten note. A text or a photo (just make sure your phone's locked, so the kids don't stumble across your private communication!). It's all about staying connected.

## Mind Your Tone

Effective communication isn't just what you say but how you say it—with both your lips and your body. In fact, researchers say that a great deal of communication is nonverbal.

We can choose whether speak kindly or harshly to someone. I remember how, when I was a kid, my mom might be straightening me out for something I had done wrong when the phone would ring, and she would answer and be all nice and warm to the person on the other end.

That doesn't mean you have to be all soft and gooey. There is a time for speaking sternly but without edge. Jesus certainly didn't mince His words on occasions, but He was never unkind.

Keep in mind also that silence can be a tone, too. A no-dial tone, telling your spouse they can't connect with you.

### Watch Your Timing

If you need to have a difficult conversation, make sure you choose the best possible time for it. Don't start talking about hot-button issues like money right before bedtime—that's not going to go well. If your spouse isn't a morning person, you don't want to try to dive into something deep first thing. Agree on the best time and place for you both. Set yourselves up for success.

## SPEAKING THE TRUTH IN LOVE

After you have shut up and really listened, *then* it's your turn to talk. The Bible is filled with powerful principles for communicating in a way that leads to oneness rather than negotiation and conflict.

> *Do not let any unwholesome talk come out of your mouths, but only what is helpful for building others up according to their needs, that it may benefit those who listen . . . Get rid of all bitterness, rage and anger, brawling and slander, along with every form of malice. Be kind and compassionate to one another, forgiving each other, just as in Christ God forgave you.* —EPHESIANS 4:29; 31-32

Notice how this passage ties communication into love and forgiveness. Here are some ways to get started:

## 1) Express appreciation.

You might have some hard things to say later, but for now, try to start the conversation with something that you genuinely and positively feel grateful to your spouse for. Tell them why and how you are thankful for them.

## 2) Take responsibility for the conflict.

I'm talking about more than just confessing your sin and asking for forgiveness (although that's certainly part of this). I'm talking about accepting the fact that God has created you to be one flesh. It's not easy. We have jobs. There is stuff going on, but the two of you are one. Take ownership and responsibility for both of you. You're the same person. If you would transition that mentally everything would change in your marriage. Maybe you're not there yet? Does this level of oneness seem impossible? Hang in there. As love, forgiveness, and communication become a reality, this type of oneness will be the fruit.

**3) Share your criticism and complaining in a problem-solving context.**

Don't just come blowing in the door, hot. When you want to enter negotiations or conflict, take those critical moments and look for an opportunity to make them constructive and centered around God's best. Jesus regularly encouraged and spurred others on to love and good deeds, especially with His disciples. His Spirit lives in you and can do the same through you. "I can do all this through him who gives me strength" (Philippians 4:13).

Conflict and negotiation cycles WILL happen, but you can break them with love, forgiveness, and good communication. It doesn't mean problems go away. It means you can get to deal with them in a way that creates oneness rather than division. Trust me, Cindy and I have been there.

Just a year or two into our marriage, I pulled off a doozie. We should have H.A.L.T.ed because I was getting angry, and neither of us was actively listening at all. Finally, I let it fly.

"If you wanted your husband to be like your dad, you should have married him!"

I asked her forgiveness immediately, but it was a couple of days before Cindy came around. It took a while before she could release this. But we lived to fight another day.

One of them came a few years ago. There was a person in our church who had really been hurting me. I felt like he was ripping my guts out and dumping a truckload of salt over everything. Then one night, Cindy and I tipped over into the conflict cycle, and she pulled out the big guns.

"Now I know why Bill is always so mad at you! Now I know why he hates you!"

That was the worst, most damaging phrase that I had ever heard in my life. She used my enemy to justify why she should hate me too? Oh, man. It tore me up. I walked away certain that our relationship could never be repaired.

But before the sun went down, she came to me and asked me for my forgiveness. She was in tears and broken over it, but it was one of those moments where you think, *That's it, we're done.* By God's grace, I was able to forgive her.

We're not done, though. And neither are you. However, God is in this with you and your spouse, and the three of you can find a better way. "Because of the LORD's great love we are not consumed, for his compassions never fail. They are new every morning; great is your faithfulness. I say to myself, 'The LORD is my portion; therefore I will wait for him'" (Lamentations 3:22-24).

## SWITCHING THINGS UP

Somebody once defined insanity as doing the same thing over and over and expecting a different result.

Are *you* insane?

You'll probably say no, but remember that nothing is going to change in your marriage if you keep doing the same thing over and over. If you don't switch it up, you're going to *stay* in that cycle of rejection and conflict.

Do you believe that you are created in God's image? Scripture says you are. Do you believe the Spirit of God lives in you? Scripture says He does. Don't diss the way that He has created you. Don't diss what He has put in you. Things can change if you trust in Him and are willing to do things differently.

Doing it differently will feel uncomfortable, awkward, and maybe even silly at first. But are you willing to quit doing the same thing over and over so that you can get a different result? Are you willing to switch it up so "that your love may abound more and more in knowledge and depth of insight"?

Here's a great way to gain some real perspective on your communication skills (or lack thereof): Record your next difficult conversation!

We got this idea from our counselor. Don't do it secretly; you're not trying to catch your partner out. Next time you're stepping into what might be a difficult conversation, ask their permission ahead of time and then hit the record button on your phone's app. It's amazing how helpful this can be, for several reasons.

First, it makes you more careful about what you say and how you say it when you know every word is being caught on tape.

Second, it reveals just how unclear our communication can be. I remember one time being adamant that I had said such-and-such to Cindy, only to discover in playback I had not. Very humbling.

The point of this is not to win a he-said, she-said argument but to help you both win by seeing where and how misunderstandings and miscommunication can occur.

Another idea is to write it out. There was a time when Cindy was trying to tell me about five major issues in our relationship that she felt were urgent. They weren't eternal, necessarily, but they were immediate, and I just wasn't listening. So she did something brilliant. She typed out the five things she was trying to say in an email. I received that email, and through that piece of communication, I was able to see so clearly exactly what she was trying to say. I let it soak in for about thirty minutes, took a breath, called her and said, "You're exactly right; I'm an idiot." And that part was really true, I can promise you that. By switching to writing, Cindy helped me to shut up and listen. I had to ask myself, "Was I really arguing over these five things?"

Finally, seek out a solid mediator/counselor. Satan is a liar. I think one of his most effective lies is convincing Christians that they're supposed to have their act together. That turns *us* into liars. We run around faking everything, pretending that we're strong and independent. It's better to be honest, genuine, and transparent. I'm not saying you throw all your marriage junk out there on Main Street for everyone to see, but you do need to be honest with somebody safe. For Cindy and me, that somebody has been Dr. Jonathan Cude, a licensed Christian counselor in Dallas.

I don't care that some people might think that means we are weak. I *am* weak! We are *all* weak in *all* sorts of ways. Everybody gets professional advice from doctors, professors, lawyers, realtors, mechanics, etc. Only pride, and Satan's lie, keep us from seeking counsel in the most important area of our lives: relationships. To be clear, I'm talking about healthy, biblically based intervention. I'm not talking about some soft-serve, tell-me-what-I-want-to-hear, feel-good stuff. We pay good money to get solid, godly counsel. And it's worth every penny because our marriage is worth it.

So is yours.

Every marriage is worth the investment of good communication. God has revealed how, and He is waiting to switch things up for you and your spouse if you will just let Him.

We can't conclude a section on communication without addressing one area of communication that gets overlooked a lot: praying together. There's such power and unity in coming before God together as a couple, but not many Christian husbands and wives do so regularly, as far as I can tell.

Maybe that's because they don't pray much on their own. You can't be something before God with your spouse that you're not with Him when it is just the two of you. Intimacy with God will flow into intimacy in our other relationships. I know many couples who have started to pray together after being at one of our conferences who have later told us what a game-changer it has been in their marriage.

Let me challenge you to start praying with your spouse if you don't. Take baby steps. Maybe start just by reading Scripture over each other—remember, the Bible is powerful and effective, And, guys, we are instructed to wash our wives with God's word (Ephesians 5:26).

Let's pray:

> *Dear God,*
> *I ask that my marriage would abound more and more in love through knowledge and insight. Convict me about my role in the negotiation/conflict cycle. In the name of Jesus, by the power of the Spirit in me, I believe that I am a great communicator. Make me willing to H.A.L.T. when I need to. Give me a listening heart. Speak the truth through me in love.*
> *Amen.*

## A HEART CHECKUP: COMMUNICATION

Great communication with your spouse starts with great communication with your Creator. Because of the cross, a personal relationship with God is possible through Christ and the Holy Spirit, and the same principles of communication apply!

- Get alone with the Lord—and then just shut up for a while. Give your brain a rest, even if just for a few minutes. Ask God to clear your thoughts so you can really hear what He wants to say to you.
- Listen to what God is saying to you in Ephesians 4. Read and ponder the whole chapter a couple of times. Write a note back to Him restating what you sense He is telling you.

- Talk with Him about what is on your heart. Ask Him to break the cycles of negotiation and conflict in your marriage and to build a new level of oneness where your love abounds more and more in knowledge and insight.
- Follow His lead as he points you to new and different things He wants you to do in your communication.
- Give those things to the Lord and trust that He will do it through you in His strength. You can do all things through Christ who strengthens you!

## TAKING YOUR COMMUNICATION TO THE NEXT LEVEL

Plan on mixing it up! We are all about breaking cycles and doing things differently, so maybe consider a different location for your next heart-to-heart: go somewhere you have never been as a couple. Maybe a campground or a zoo or an amusement park.

- Rehearse the H.A.L.T. strategy by sharing how Hunger, Anger, Loneliness, and Tiredness affect your communication. Pick out a couple of the "magic phrases" that you think will be appropriate when the two of you find yourself veering toward the negotiation/conflict cycle. You might want to add a few phrases of your own. Practice saying them to each other. Make a commitment to respect the other person's wishes when they call for a "time out."

- Read Philippians 1:1-11 together. Highlight or underline the phrases that are most important to you as a couple. What is God trying to say to you?
- Brainstorm on new ways the two of you can communicate. What do you think about using recordings? What if you started writing letters and notes? How could you use social media? Pick one new way to start with and give it a try!
- Discuss where you can find a good mediator or counselor. What would be some of the advantages of connecting with someone like that?
- Hold hands and pray (silently or out loud) through Philippians 1:9-11. Make it *your* prayer for *your* marriage.

# CHAPTER FOUR
# THE HEART OF MARRIAGE

## Chamber IV: Red-Hot Sex

*The L*ORD *God said, "It is not good for the man to be alone"*
*. . . That is why a man leaves his father and mother and*
*is united to his wife, and they become one flesh. Adam*
*and his wife were both naked, and they felt no shame.*
—GENESIS 2:18, 24-25

I love my job almost all the time. There are weeks where I definitely earn my paycheck, but for the most part, I get paid to have a front-row seat to watch God change lives. One of the most amazing things I get to see is when marriages catch fire at our Romance Uncensored events and conferences.

It's really a shame what has happened to sex. I'm not talking about sex on the internet, on the streets, or in the entertainment industry; I'm talking about sex in Christianity. For some reason, sex has gotten majorly censored in the church. Nobody really talks about it unless it's all negative or unless it's the junk we are all supposed *not* to do: D*on't have an affair. Don't look at pornography. Don't have sex before marriage. Don't lust.* Avoid all those things and then we are living in God's will, right?

Not in my mind. The church has done a good job teaching purity and a poor job at teaching marital passion. Remember the True Love Waits movement of some years back, with all the pledges and purity rings? That was helpful as far as it went. However, some Christians who embraced that have been married for years and they are still waiting . . . to experience true sexual intimacy because they were never taught how. They didn't hear that sex as God intended is a form of worship. He created it, so we can participate in intimate worship with our spouse.

In the beginning, God created us male and female. He designed us for oneness in *every* way. Yes, that includes emotional and spiritual stuff, but come on! The most obvious part of his design for oneness is physical. The male and female bodies were created to be smooshed together in a hormone-injected, turbo-passionate, ultra-intense embrace. "Naked and unashamed" all wrapped up together until you can't tell where one person ends and the other one starts, so they become "one flesh."

That's the biblical design. But when Adam and Eve turned from God's perfect plan back in the Garden of Eden, their immediate response was to hide themselves from each other with clothing and then to hide from God Himself. When they deviated from His plan, their sexuality became taboo and shameful. And we have been censoring the topic of sex ever since. Worst of all, because of Satan's lies, we've created a mental, emotional, and spiritual barrier between sex and God—and it's robbing us. Instead of sex being worship in marriage, we worship sex outside of marriage.

I know life is never going to be perfect like it was in the garden. But I say it's time to tell Satan to go to hell and to begin to reclaim and pursue the sexual heaven that God created us to experience on this earth. I say it's time to *un*-censor romance and talk openly and boldly about God, sexuality, and the scriptures.

## THE GOD/SEX BARRIER

If there is any question in your mind that God intended sex to be free, frequent, pleasurable, and highly erotic, look no further than the Bible. The Song of Solomon is devoted almost entirely to sex. Some theologians have tried to explain it away as being a literary metaphor for God's love for the church. Sure, there are some verses in that book that *can* be interpreted that way, but gimme a break: This book of the Bible is a steamy hot love letter. The whole first chapter is clearly about sexual foreplay. Consider these passages, for example:

> *"Let him kiss me with the kisses of his mouth— for your love is more delightful than wine . . . Take me away with you—let us hurry! Let the king bring me into his chambers . . . While the king was at his table, my perfume spread its fragrance. My beloved is to me a sachet of myrrh resting between my breasts. My beloved is to me a cluster of henna blossoms from the vineyards of En Gedi."* —SONG OF SOLOMON 1:2, 4, 12-14

I don't know what a sachet of myrrh or a henna blossom is, and I've never been to the vineyards of En Gedi, but if Cindy is into it, I'd love to find out some night . . . you know, just to follow what the Bible says!

It's tastefully written, but this is X-rated stuff. One chapter later, Solomon's bride even describes the two of them in a heavy petting situation and warns other women not to go there until they're ready because they probably won't be able to stop:

> *"His left arm is under my head, and his right arm embraces me. Daughters of Jerusalem, I charge you by the gazelles*

*and by the does of the field: Do not arouse or awaken love*
*until it so desires."* —SONG OF SOLOMON 2:6-7

This isn't just a part-A-connects-with-part-B manual. One of the problems with the world's view of sex is that it's been reduced to a matter of mechanics. But true sexual intimacy isn't just about our bodies; it involves our hearts.

Notice that the whole encounter begins with loving words of affirmation, adoration, and affection. There's tons of practical advice in here. No joke, you get a couple of paragraphs into this book and you're either going to need a cold shower or you're going to need to find your spouse fast. This is kindling and fuel for burning-hot passion between a husband and a wife. Song of Solomon even talks about how to create an irresistible erotic environment. And it includes some crazy anatomical descriptions for sexual body parts, and it does so without any shame . . . but I'm getting ahead of myself. The point I'm trying to make is simply this:

Our holy God wanted a steamy hot love letter in the Holy Scriptures because a red-hot sexual marriage is holy.

Seriously, who do you think invented sex in the first place?

*The LORD God said, "It is not good for the man to be alone"*
*. . . So the LORD God caused the man to fall into a deep*

> *sleep; and while he was sleeping, he took one of the man's ribs and then closed up the place with flesh. Then the LORD God made a woman from the rib he had taken out of the man, and he brought her to the man. The man said, "This is now bone of my bones and flesh of my flesh; she shall be called 'woman,' for she was taken out of man." That is why a man leaves his father and mother and is united to his wife, and they become one flesh. Adam and his wife were both naked, and they felt no shame.* —GENESIS 2:18, 21-25

*One flesh, naked, no shame*, that's God's design. (Jesus even quoted this passage in Matthew 19 and Mark 10. Paul quoted it in 1 Corinthians 6 and Ephesians 5.) That deserves more than a head nod or a golf clap. That deserves a full-on hallelujah, stand up and jump up and down, and praise the Lord. I'm telling you, if you want to get into sex, get into God's Word, the way He designed it.

> *May your fountain be blessed, and may you rejoice in the wife of your youth. A loving doe, a graceful deer—may her breasts satisfy you always, may you ever be intoxicated with her love.* —PROVERBS 5:18-19

If you look at the verses around this one, God is openly talking about breasts, semen, and pheromones—and He's saying we should get drunk with it. Bring it on! What breaks my heart is how many couples operate in an institution that

God created (marriage) without even having God involved. It's really foolish to think that we would be a part of an institution and never ask the designer's opinion or investigate what He says about it.

If we don't embrace the sexual as sacred, you are going to think it is forbidden, and how you think about sex is the kind of sex you're going to have. If you think stolen sex is good, you're going to be addicted to porn, be tempted to find release from someone besides your spouse, probably get addicted to someone else's emotions, and set yourself up for divorce.

## CONNECTING THE SEXUAL AND SACRED

One of the best anniversary gifts Cindy has given me was a bedroom makeover. She bought a bunch of battery-powered candles and little trees with lights all over them. Then she had a friend come over and repaint the entire bedroom. To top it off, she stenciled this beautiful phrase on our back wall: "With you I am complete . . . With you I have everything."

She changed it all, creating a sacred space where we can celebrate being one flesh. Is your bedroom like that? Go to your bedroom mentally right now and look at it. What do you see in your mind? How does it make you feel?

Take some advice from Solomon and create surroundings that are blistering, beautiful, and hot. Let's start by clearing some stuff out of the way:

- The computer
- The crib
- The mail
- The laundry
- The desk

You need to get that stuff out of there. You've got better things to do in that space. The bedroom is not the place for Facebook, business, news, or chore lists. God says the marriage bed should stay *pure*. So, clear out the junk and replace it with things that can transform that room into a place where the sacred and the sexual come together as God intended.

While we're talking about what to leave out of the bedroom, let's add conflict to the list. As I said earlier, good communication means being able to have hard conversations in a healthy way, but aim to have those somewhere else, so you always think of your bedroom as a place where you are celebrating your differences, not discussing them!

After all, it's not just a bedroom; it's a sanctuary, a cathedral, and a chapel. Why? Because sex is *worship*.

Sorry, did I just enter the weird zone? Well, think about it:

> *Or do you not know that your body is a temple of the Holy Spirit who is in you, whom you have from God, and that you are not your own?* —1 CORINTHIANS 6:19 (NKJV)

> *Therefore I urge you, brethren, by the mercies of God, to present your bodies a living and holy sacrifice, acceptable to God, which is your spiritual service of worship.* —ROMANS 12:1 (NASB95)

> *Marriage should be honored by all, and the marriage bed kept pure . . .* —HEBREWS 13:4

God isn't just into sex as the One who created it and designed it. He is actually into you. If you've asked Him into your life, His Spirit resides in your spirit, making your fleshly body a temple of worship.

With that in mind, I'm going to suggest you replace that bedside table you may have; you know, the one probably cluttered with a bunch of junk. Either clear it off or, if you don't have one, buy one of those little wooden ones and lay a nice piece of cloth over it. Then, as a couple, place a few things on it that will remind you that your bedroom is a sacred place of intimate worship for you and your spouse:

- Candles
- Oil (often used in the Bible for anointing and healing)
- Incense
- Love letters
- Speakers and an iPhone full of "worship" music.

Oh, and make sure there's a lock on the drawer, so your kids don't take this stuff out and show it to their friends.

Most importantly, remove all insecurities and become vulnerable, with no separation between the sacred and the sexual, when you come together as God intended.

Jesus did this for you. He died on the cross for you, naked and unashamed. He gave His life for you. Now, with hearts full of worship and praise, give yourself unashamedly to your spouse.

## TAKING CARE OF YOURSELF

When Adam and Eve chose to do things their own way, a lot of things got messed up. Getting things right with God and realizing the sacredness of sex is a huge step in rediscovering His original design for intimacy on all levels. But that doesn't mean that all sexual struggles are going to disappear magically. Some will need to be faced with patience and persistence, but it is worth it. Remember that sex is a mandate in a healthy Christ-centered marriage:

*Do not deprive each other except perhaps by mutual consent and for a time, so that you may devote yourselves to prayer. Then come together again so that Satan will not tempt you because of your lack of self-control.* —1 CORINTHIANS 7:5

Sex is definitely a physical act, and when our human physique isn't functioning perfectly, it can be a barrier to sex. I'm not a medical physician, but I do know that medications can have a big impact on our level of sexual desire and performance. They can make it difficult for a guy to have an erection or kill a woman's emotional sexual desires. So, take a close look at your hormone medication. Maybe reconsider your depression medications. Get a second opinion. Find out if you really need them. Some of that stuff really messes up your sex life.

It's no surprise that age takes a toll on your physical body as well. Between the ages of forty and fifty-five, women go through "menopause" (I call it men-on-pause), and some men go through "andropause" when hormones shift, and sexual drive and stamina can change. If you suspect a physical issue, talk to a qualified professional. Oftentimes they can help. Certain medications are making a vibrant sex life possible decades longer than in the past.

In some cases, physical problems make intercourse impossible. But that doesn't mean your sex life dies. You and your spouse can experience orgasm without having intercourse. There are so many ways that you can pleasure each other and share physical intimacy "until death do you part," regardless of physical limitations. If you've got challenges, talk about them first with your spouse and then with someone who can help.

A few years back, Cindy told me, "Shannon, I think you are made for CrossFit." (Translation: "You need to lose weight.") At first, I was a bit offended, but when I looked in the mirror, I had to concede she was right. There was the Pillsbury Doughboy, staring back at me. Physical appearance isn't everything, of course, but it is something, and I'm fortunate that when I married Cindy, I got a real-life Barbie.

So I told her I would pray about it, and then I committed to 90 days. Some eight years later, I am still at it. Cindy was right: I love everything about CrossFit and the blessing it has been in so many ways. I've lost around seventy pounds, and I have got so much more energy for everything—and I mean, everything (insert smiley face!).

When your body is out of shape, your sex life can whither. It's all about the blood flow. If you don't keep your heart pumping as it should, your sexual stamina can suffer. But getting in shape is also great for your mind and your communication. Start exercising and eating right as a couple. And if you need a new incentive to do a workout video, try it together with the door locked and the lights down low. You never know what might happen ...

It's also worth keeping in mind that the Bible says our bodies are the temple of the Holy Spirit (1 Corinthians 6:19). In the Old Testament, there were stringent rules for how the temple—the place of God's most intimate presence—should be treated. When I started to get more in shape, I realized how, without realizing it, I had been undermining some of my effectiveness as a preacher. I may have been talking about what God's Word said, but I wasn't displaying discipline in my life. People could tell just by looking at me that I lacked self-control. Now that I am somewhat fitter and healthier, I believe my words carry more weight because I am lighter!

Even in a good marriage, it's easy to get lackadaisical with things that can throw a damper on our sex life. A couple of suggestions:

Guys, the gold-and-blue-band whitey-tighties need to go. There ain't nobody that needs to be wearing that underwear to bed. And, ladies, it's time to burn the grannie-panties. You know what I'm talking about. Your mom wore them, and so did her mom's mom. Time to break the chain and find something silky and smooth. You are worth it, and he will appreciate it. And if anything either of you wears has holes or marks in 'em, throw 'em in the trash! They may be your favorites, but they are probably not his/hers! You may be laughing, but you know it's real.

I know there are plenty of things that you can't change, but your mate will appreciate it if you change the things you can to make a difference to them. A shave, a shower, and a little bit of cologne or perfume can make a big difference. Guys, if she doesn't like the hair on your back, Nair works—but don't use that stuff on your privates. I had a friend who went on a cruise and Nair'd some inappropriate areas. He never saw the ocean: Five days in the infirmary!

## YOUR OTHER SEX ORGANS

Healthy sex isn't just about taking care of your physical body. The heart (as the seat of your emotions, not the blood pumper) and mind are indispensable sex organs. If either of those is in the wrong place, your sex life won't be in the right place. Particularly when a marriage has cooled off or is going through tough times, it is so tempting to seek emotional intimacy somewhere else.

That's why, men, you have to have an eye to where your wife works, if she does work. I'm not saying you should be some crazy man with a shotgun, but she does need to know that you are protecting her. There is no greater intimacy than her knowing you're protecting her from working in a tempting environment where some dude is playing to her emotional needs. Does your wife have to work in some place where some guy will be hitting on her every day so that she can bring in a few extra dollars so you can make an extra payment on cable TV, the car you want, or a hunting lease?

It's the same trap for both genders. Wanting more stuff means more work and more temptation that can kill your sex life and your marriage. It's crazy, but advertisers are spending billions to convince you that if you buy their stuff, sex comes with it: Beer, cars, clothes, perfume—you name it. They try to sell it all with the promise of sex. But isn't all that junk a distraction from good sex as God designed it? Forget the stuff. Go for the priceless things.

We have all heard that familiarity breeds contempt, but sex was not designed to be boring. Variety is the spice of life, and I serve a God who is endlessly creative! After two decades of marriage, I thought maybe Cindy and I had tried everything. But then we had one of the best dates of our lives. We got on a four-wheeler and went exploring. I'm not going to say exactly what we explored or how we were sitting on the four-wheeler, but I can tell you that I can drive one of those things sitting backward. That's all I'm saying about that, but the point is that a little creativity destroys boredom. New music, new positions, new places, new schedules . . . as long as you are both into it, go for it.

What other things does your mate like? Maybe you could mix it up with that? Knitting? Kart racing? Romantic chick flicks? The football playoffs? Think about it, then shock them with your thoughtful creativity. Just look around. What could you do with a can of whipped cream or a carton of cake sprinkles?

The number one complaint that Cindy and I hear from women is that their husbands don't talk very much. The first question I always ask them is, "How often do you give him hot sex?" They don't seem to see the connection.

What's the number one complaint from men? "My wife doesn't want to have sex very much." The first question I always ask them is, "How often do you really communicate your love to her?" Just like their wives, they don't see the connection.

I don't think there's anything that launches a marriage into the negotiating/conflict spiral like sex and communication. The question is this: What really comes first, good sex or good communication? Many women say they need to feel connected for good sex. Many guys say good sex makes them feel connected.

The reality is it's not either/or. It's both/and. Sexual intimacy creates great communication. Great communication creates great sexual intimacy.

And either partner can make the first move when they allow the love of Christ to move through them. In love, both partners should make the first move on a regular basis.

In the ideal situation, both partners are trusting in Christ to love the other person through them and forgiving the other person when they don't live up to their expectations. If both of you are initiating good communication, and setting the stage for great sex, the negotiation/conflict cycle won't even get started. But if both of you get selfish and start withholding love from your mate, it's a disaster in the making.

You need to create a level of intimacy expectation:

- Call, text, maybe Snapchat each other throughout the day.
- Buy a new piece of lingerie, or flowers, and sneak them into your mate's purse or briefcase.
- Dump the kids for the evening and go out to dinner or have just a special dinner alone at home.
- Find a new and clear way to share your desires and expectations.
- Get cleaned up and dress for the occasion.
- Write notes to each other.

The possibilities are endless. Do anything and everything to create healthy communication and sexual expectation. And your love will take care of the rest.

# A HEART CHECKUP: RED-HOT SEX

If you're willing to do what it takes to break through the barriers to awesome sexual intimacy, your marriage can become red-hot. And you know what? The world doesn't know what to do with that kind of a marriage. I often wear a shirt with "My wife is hot" on the front. No one knows what to do with that shirt. Both men and women will ask, "Did she buy that for ya? Hahahaha!"

"No," I tell them. "I paid for it myself. Matter of fact, I made it."

They're like, "Ohhhhh . . ."

I'm not suggesting everybody gets a shirt like that—if you do, I'll need to come up with something else to let Cindy know my love for her is unique and intense. So, come up with some stuff of your own, okay? And if your sex life needs a tune-up, or if it's broken and you don't know how to fix it, I'm telling you to get help from the right place.

Marriage retreats are a great place to start. Most churches have them. Other organizations offer them. Most mediators and counselors are used to helping couples with sex. If you sit with an expert (and someone who is well-grounded in the Word), huge problems can often be resolved easily. One couple came into a counseling center with really significant negotiation/conflict issues. They dug down through a decade of issues, but at the bottom, the counselor discovered that the wife had never experienced an orgasm. She felt continually used in bed and deeply resented it. They were a "good Christian" couple and had never talked to anyone about it. The counselor explained just a few details of female anatomy, and WOW! It broke the negotiation/conflict cycle and lit the fire for a red-hot marriage.

All four chambers of the heart need to be pumping well for a healthy marriage. When one is clogged, it affects all the others. But when all four are in functioning well, love, forgiveness, healthy communication, *and* hot, regular sex create a marriage that can powerfully display the love of Christ to the world.

Christ has promised that He will always be with you and that He will never leave you (Hebrews 13:5). God knows your thoughts; He knows your desires . . . He just knows! It's time to get alone with Him and finally get completely real with Him about sex. You can't tell Him anything that He doesn't already know. You don't have any desires or frustrations that He is not aware of. And there's a good chance that you've let the lies of Satan and the results of the fall compartmentalize your sexuality from the sacredness of God.

- *Ponder.* Spend some time meditating on the Song of Solomon. Imagine that he is describing you and your spouse.
- *Pray.* Pour out your heart: Ask the Holy Spirit to search your heart and to reveal areas and issues of your sexuality

that you have never openly communicated to God. You might need to confess some things that nobody else knows about. Whatever it is that's on your heart, talk to Him about it. He will never forsake you, nor will He ever reject you. His forgiveness flows to every area of your life. You may have frustrations that you've been embarrassed to tell Him about. Tell Him everything right now. You may have never asked Him to be the central focus of your sexual relationship with your spouse. Talk to Him about that.

- *Listen.* From what you have read in His Word and what He is revealing to your spirit, what is He telling you about sex and worship? What else is He speaking to you? Talk to Him about it!

- *Share.* Bring what you have learned to your spouse. This may sound crazy at first but find somewhere you can talk together that is in a fairly public place. *Huh?* you may be thinking. You'll want to be sure no one can overhear you, of course! But being away from home keeps your space there a sacred sanctuary and being out in public together will help ensure you're really careful about how you talk about your sexual intimacy, with gentleness and grace.

- Go back through this chapter and talk about whatever seems to be most important to each of you.

- Share anything important from your personal time with Jesus.

- What might be the advantages of going to a marriage conference or retreat?
- What would it be like to go through one of the resources listed at the end of this chapter?
- Are there any stubborn issues that you think could be helped by a mediator or a counselor?
- Reread the section about transforming your bedroom into a place of worship and preparing a bedside table. What particular things would you want there to symbolize the sacredness of your sexuality?
- Next, work together to buy anything you want to transform your bedroom together. Get ready to do it right! Light the candles, turn on the music, and wear your favorites.
- Together, kneeling at that table you have prepared, read your favorite passage from the Song of Solomon, then make some new vows to each other!

Husband: "I commit my body to you free of shame, wholly yours, taking care of my temple for your utmost pleasure as worship to our God, in the name of the Father, in the name of the Son, in the name of the Holy Spirit."

Wife: "I was created for you, sexually, to meet your needs and to be your joy. I commit now to pleasure you and no one else for the rest of our lives. Take me now; I'm yours. In the name of the Father, the Son, and the Holy Spirit."

Amen and amen!

## CHAPTER FIVE

# THE HEART OF PARENTING

## Chamber I: Love

*See what great love the Father has lavished on us, that we should be called children of God! And that is what we are! . . . Dear friends, now we are children of God, and what we will be has not yet been made known. But we know that when Christ appears, we shall be like him, for we shall see him as he is.*
—1 JOHN 3:1-2

There are few things more intimate than eating dinner with people you value, honor, and desire . . . and there is no one I value, honor, and desire more than my family. Sometimes, when we've been at the table, I've wished I could just sit back in my chair and soak it all in. I wished I could take a 3-D photograph and freeze-frame some of the moments together. I have loved hearing my children laugh and tell stories and say, "Mom, that is the best I've ever had!" I have loved talking about our days and what they learned at school, and holding hands and giving thanks for all He has done . . . Man, I'm telling you, those were busy, chaotic years in our house, but when everybody was seated around the table face-to-face, everything in the world just seemed right, even if for just a few minutes.

One night I sat back and watched one of my girls decorate one of my favorite desserts: chocolate cake—just plain old chocolate cake out of the box. I don't know if there's anything better on planet Earth. She made it and decorated it just right (and somehow mixed in a bunch of love.) Then she set it in the middle of the table ready to serve . . . that's about as close to heaven as you can get on earth. When all is well with your family, all else seems good too.

But I have a word of caution here. Yes, a healthy family can be a glimpse of heaven, but we need to keep things in perspective. Some churches talk about "family first," which is an overemphasis. Nowhere does the Bible tell us to put family first. No, we are told to put God first. "Seek the Kingdom of God above all else" (Matthew 6:33, NLT), and then everything else falls into place.

So how do we seek His kingdom first? We seek to love like Jesus.

It's amazing how much love permeates the New Testament. Once Jesus came on the scene, love took the spotlight in new ways. How do we let love permeates our home and our parenting?

Love Jesus.

It's that simple. No reason to overcomplicate things. If you love Him with real love, everything else will follow. But it's got to be real love. Not just some sentimental head-nod. It's loving Jesus with all your heart, soul, mind, and strength.

When you love somebody, you love what they love. For example, the Holy Spirit recently led me to buy a new bow. (I tend to sense this leading of God every fall, just before hunting season; and, yes, I'm joking), I know it was the Lord, yet when I showed it to Cindy, she was like, "You get suckered into a new bow every year!"

No, no, she didn't actually say that (but I could tell by the slight roll of her eyes that that's what she was thinking.) She paused, took a little breath, and said, "Let me see!" I showed her all the stuff on it that I loved, and she acted like she genuinely cared. To her, I'm sure it looked just like the bow the Spirit told me to buy last year, but she loved that bow too because she loved me and knew I loved it.

The point is simply this: if you love Jesus, you're going to love what He loves.

> *Jesus replied, "Anyone who loves me will obey my teaching. My Father will love them, and we will come to them and make our home with them. Anyone who does not love me will not obey my teaching. These words you hear are not my own; they belong to the Father who sent me."*
> —JOHN 14:23-24

If we love Him and love what He does, our children will pick up on that. But it's not just for example or for show for your kids. Search your heart and make sure it's the real thing that you love because He first loved you, and that it's His love overflowing out of you.

There are tons of ways that you can instill this love in your kids. We'll get to that in just a little bit, but first of all, let's take a reality pill.

## WHEN FAMILY FEELS FRACTURED

Life is good when things are going well. But life is not all chocolate cake. Family can be a place of bitterness and disappointment.

When you genuinely love your kids, you're going to be vulnerable. You can't love without exposing yourself to the possibility of getting hurt and things going really wrong. The people who will betray you the worst are the ones seated at the table close enough to kiss you. That's one of the risks of love: You open yourself up to be wounded. Scripture is full of examples of what can go wrong around the family table. Adam and Eve, Jacob and Esau, Joseph his brothers, and there's plenty more.

When you open up your heart in the home, your spouse, your kids, and even strangers you have welcomed will be close enough to kick you in the shins or even stab you in the back while smiling at you. Big ouch. I'm telling you it's going to happen. It happened to Jesus, and it's going to happen to us. Think about it. Jesus had spent three years with the disciples. By this point in his ministry, the disciples were like family . . . and yet Judas betrayed Him *to the death* for a fistful of silver:

> *In the same way, after the supper he took the cup, saying,*
> *"This cup is the new covenant in my blood, which is poured*
> *out for you. But the hand of him who is going to betray*
> *me is with mine on the table. The Son of Man will go as it*
> *has been decreed. But woe to that man who betrays him!"*
> —LUKE 22:20-22

Some people feel that betrayal is the worst kind of wound, and I agree. You rarely see it coming. It's probably the closeness and the caring that makes its impact so much greater. Other than our spouses, there's probably nobody closer and nobody we care about more than our kids. When things go wrong with them, or worse yet, when they walk away, we take the wound.

What happens when your kids don't do what you think they should do? What happens when your kid doesn't turn out to be a doctor, a lawyer, the president, or a missionary to Russia? What happens when you give your kids your all and then it seems like you've lost them? You think to yourself, What happened? What's going on here?

I don't know about you, but I want to hear from God's Word concerning that issue because many of us have felt the guilt, we've felt the blame, we've felt the pain when our child goes on the run. Or maybe you're a child of God and you feel like you're on the run and think God won't forgive you? Either way, Jesus has a story for you in Luke chapter 15. It goes something like this:

> *There was a man who had two sons, and he loved them like they were his own sons because, well, they were. The younger one was the one who lived on the edge, and one day he decided to cross the line for good. "Father, give me my share of the estate." So the father divided his property between them. Soon, the younger son got took the cash and he jetted. He set off for a distant country where he*

*partied like crazy and blew it all.* —LUKE 15:1-13, (SOV, SHANNON O'DELL VERSION)

Chances are, in one way or another, you're going to have a "prodigal" someday.

What are some evidences that your son or daughter is on the run?

*Number one: Self-centeredness.* Babies and toddlers think only of themselves, but when an older kid acts like that all the time, and others in God don't matter, you have got a prodigal at heart.

*Number two: Know-it-all.* Prodigals think they have all the answers. Don't bother offering advice or arguing with them. They honestly think you're as dumb as a brick.

*Number three: Immediate gratification.* When you see your child wanting what they want, when they want it, there's a prodigal spirit in there. And in order to get what they want, they will squander the riches of God's grace, the riches of your family, and the riches of your love.

Prodigals display these symptoms in an incredible variety of ways across a broad range of intensity. Responding to and treating these symptoms is as much an art as it is a science. If there were some magic formula that could make them all right again, I'd be glad to write the book and make millions. But simplistic answers simply don't exist. I know this firsthand because I've lived it. I have loved the beauty of watching my kids grow into who and what God created them to be. But sometimes, it was tough. There were times when I just flat-out cried or shouted out, because it hurts when a prodigal is giving you fits. So what do you do?

There is plenty of wisdom to be gathered from those who've gone before us, and the Word of God is filled with eternally significant examples and guidance. Let's start there, on our knees:

### 1) Pray for humility.

If you've got a prodigal son or daughter, the most important thing you can do at the beginning is to recognize that all of us were *and still are* prodigals. You might as well humble yourself right now, because that's probably one of the gracious reasons God is allowing your kid to go off the deep end. I was a nine-year-old prodigal and on the run. But from the end of road, I saw my heavenly Father through the person of Jesus Christ, and He redeemed me and forgave me of my prodigal ways in March of 1981. But that spirit of self-centeredness and know-it-all, immediate gratification is alive and well in my flesh today. It's only by God's grace and by the power of His Spirit in me that I can walk the line. So, when I see my kids crossing the line? I better be humble about it. So should you. Yes, we are parents, but we are first and foremost children—children of God.

> *See what great love the Father has lavished on us, that we should be called children of God! And that is what we are! . . . Dear friends, now we are children of God, and what we will be has not yet been made known. But we know that when Christ appears, we shall be like him, for we shall see him as he is.* —1 JOHN 3:1-2

As God's kids, we are all excitable. God is still transforming us, showing we are "capable of being awakened, aroused or stirred up to action." Our souls, too, can be ignited when we experience the love of God. That's why, in parenting, there is nothing more important than humbling yourself and getting serious with God. When you understand His love, you'll understand better how to love your kids. "Follow God's example, therefore, as dearly loved children and walk in the way of love, just as Christ loved us and gave himself up for us as a fragrant offering and sacrifice to God" (Ephesians 5:1-2).

God's love is tough sometimes. Jesus says, "Those whom I love I rebuke and discipline. So be earnest and repent" (Revelation 3:19). Most people haven't memorized *that* part of the passage! Our love for our prodigal will need to include "rebuke and discipline," too, but it only works if it comes from that humble spirit of a parent who recognizes they too are a child.

### 2) Be gracious to yourself.

Sure, you may not have done the greatest job as a parent. But ultimately, our children are responsible for the choices they make in life. Jesus was perfect in every way and poured into the lives of His twelve closest friends, but one of them ended up walking away.

### 3) Pray with transparency.

That is, we should let our kids see and hear our prayers, and they should be able to see through our words to the love of God in us. We should be praying with our kids and over our kids. Paul gives us a great list to get started:

> *For this reason, since the day we heard about you, we have not stopped praying for you. We continually ask God to fill you with the knowledge of his will through all the wisdom and understanding that the Spirit gives, so that you may live a life worthy of the Lord and please him in every way: bearing fruit in every good work, growing in the knowledge of God, being strengthened with all power according to his glorious might so that you may have great endurance and patience, and giving joyful thanks to the Father, who*

*has qualified you to share in the inheritance of his holy people in the kingdom of light.* —COLOSSIANS 1:9-12

I think it's great to pray these things when you're together at the table, whether that's at breakfast or bedtime—you've got your kid captive.

### 4) Pray that they'll get caught when they're guilty.

I know that sounds ugly, but for a prodigal, experience isn't just the best teacher; sometimes it's the *only* teacher that can get through. Check out what David wrote about himself in the Psalms 119:67, 71-72: "Before I was afflicted I went astray, but now I obey your word . . . It was good for me to be afflicted so that I might learn your decrees . . . The law from your mouth is more precious to me than thousands of pieces of silver and gold."

Rather than try to save our kids from the pain of their actions, it's almost always best to let them learn the hard way, particularly if they are know-it-alls. Ask God to rattle their cage and get their attention! That's the only thing that got through to the prodigal son: "After he had spent everything, there was a severe famine in that whole country, and he began to be in need. So he went and hired himself out to a citizen of that country, who sent him to his fields to feed pigs. He longed to fill his stomach with the pods that the pigs were eating, but no one gave him anything" (Luke 15:14-16).

When my kids and my friends weren't walking with God, I prayed that consequences would come soon and severely. We're all too valuable to the kingdom of God to be living aloof to His principles. The sooner we get corrected and get back on track, the better.

### 5) Pray for patience and keep "scoping."

Galatians 6:9 says, "Let us not become weary in doing good...." So hang in there. In God's timing, you will reap a good harvest, but I can guarantee it's going to happen on God's timetable and not yours. That's because He is going to be working on *you* as He works on *them*. It's amazing how a prodigal can be used by the Spirit to reveal pride, arrogance, and a judgmental spirit. You'll wish He would fix your kid today, but chances are He's not done with you yet.

The key to parental success when your kid is on the run is the promise of their return. In Luke 15, the father saw his son "while he was still a long way off." The father must have been on the watch, looking into the distance like a hunter searching a forest through his scope. When my kids bombed, my natural tendency was to say, "Phhhhbb. What's the use? They're gonna do their own thing. Let 'em go and let's get back to life." Wrong response. You have to continue to hope, and continue to scope the horizon for their return.

### 6) Pray that they will come to their senses.

There have been times when—even as a child of God under the love of the Father and the compassion of His grace—that I've run like a prodigal. If you are humble, you'll admit that you have, too. But here's the deal: If you are truly a child of God, you *will* come to your senses. If your kid is God's kid, they will too. It's a promise:

> *When he came to his senses, he said, "How many of my father's hired servants have food to spare, and here I am starving to death! I will set out and go back to my father and say to him: Father, I have sinned against heaven and against you. I am no longer worthy to be called your son; make me like one of your hired servants." So he got up and went to his father.* —LUKE 15:17-20

Christ's invitation to walk together never expires. He's always there waiting to fellowship and share life again. Pray that He will allow your child to see the truth. Remember, our kids are excitable; they are "capable of being awakened, aroused, or stirred up to action," just like we are. Never stop praying that God's Spirit will give them the wake-up call.

### 7) Love them unconditionally.

Luke 15:20 tells how "while he was still a long way off, his father saw him and was filled with compassion for him; he ran to his son, threw his arms around him and kissed him." Is that not the most powerful picture? The father ran to him. And then it says, "He threw his arms around him." That kind of reception doesn't just happen. It happens because of forgiveness.

Prodigals break our expectations and dreams. They drain us and wound us at our core. Please take that to the cross of forgiveness. You'll need to walk through forgiveness with them just like you do your spouse because those who sit closest to you are the ones who can hurt you the most. And remember: The pain of the wrong and the things you have to go through will be outweighed by the joy of their return. "Therefore, as God's chosen people, holy and dearly loved, clothe yourselves with compassion, kindness, humility, gentleness and patience. Bear with each other and forgive one another if any of you has a grievance against someone. Forgive as the Lord forgave you. And over all these virtues put on love, which binds them all together in perfect unity" (Colossians 3:12-14).

### 8) Celebrate their homecoming.

But the father said to his servants, "Quick! Bring the best robe and put it on him. Put a ring on his finger and sandals on his feet. Bring the fattened calf and kill it. Let's have a feast and celebrate. For this son of mine was dead and is alive again; he was lost and is found." So they began to celebrate (Luke 15:22-24).

When the kid leaves the table, so to speak, it's appropriate, in some way, to celebrate them again when they return. Don't get me wrong. I'm not saying you just start over like nothing happened. There will be a time for "rebuke and discipline" even if they are "earnest and repent." There may be serious consequences for their behavior, but let them know that you're on their team. You need to forgive, absolutely. Celebrate even small steps in the right direction. That's what our heavenly Father does for us.

In all this, don't miss the importance of physical touch in expressing unconditional love. The prodigal son was probably pretty stinky by the time he got home, but his dad didn't hesitate to give him a big hug. Our kids need our touch. It may change as they grow, from hugs and snuggles to high-fives and fist bumps, but they need that physical expression of your love for them. If kids don't get it at home, they will go looking elsewhere for it. It's no accident that, in the Old Testament, the generational blessing was passed on with the laying on of hands.

## PLANNING TO PARENT WELL

As I said, parenting is more art than science. But it's such a beautiful process. You've been given a piece of history to shape.

You, as a child of God, are a piece of history too. God is shaping you and your family to build His kingdom. You are preparing time travelers to take the good news of the kingdom into the future, long after you are gone. We need to be sensitive to that and take it seriously! It's an incredibly important opportunity and responsibility, and love is the first and most important leg.

A couple of things you can do right now:

Order one of these awesome books that do a great job of describing the heart chamber of love in parenting:

- *How to Really Love Your Child or How to Really Love Your Teen* by Dr. Ross Campbell.
- *The Five Love Languages for Children* or *The Five Love Languages for Teens* by Gary D. Chapman.
- *Love Must Be Tough* by Dr. James Dobson.
- *Who Switched Off My Brain?* by Dr. Caroline Leaf
- *Keep Your Love On* by Danny Silk

And start praying now. Don't put this off any longer. If your child is living in your home, regardless of the age, bring 'em together and pray with them daily. Now, I understand how difficult that can be, with busy schedules and carpools and football games and work and blah blah blah. But it's time to put the excuses aside and go for it! This is one area where you can really be creative.

- Send a prayer text.
- Stick a prayer note in their binder.
- Send a prayer bomb in an email.
- Skype or Facetime or Marco Polo 'em.

And there are always those few moments at the end of the night when you tuck them in or lay a hand on their shoulder and pray God's blessings upon them.

You can pray what's on your heart or use prompts from the truth of the Bible. I regularly prayed Proverbs 1:10-12 for my kids:

> *My son, if sinful men entice you, do not give in to them. If they say, "Come along with us; let's lie in wait for innocent blood, let's ambush some harmless soul; let's swallow them alive, like the grave, and whole, like those who go down to the pit . . ."*

Sometimes I prayed Psalm 1:1-3 over them:

> *Blessed is the one who does not walk in step with the wicked or stand in the way that sinners take or sit in the company of mockers, but whose delight is in the law of the LORD, and who meditates on his law day and night. That person is like a tree planted by streams of water, which yields its fruit in season . . .*

Schedule some meaningful family time. I just beg of you, take your calendar and prioritize three meals a week at the table with your family, minimum. Three meals a week. For some, breakfast may be the best time of day. For some, it may be dinner. Or lunch out on the town. I know our schedules are demanding, but don't let someone else counter the moments that Jesus counted so important. If you do not calendar your time, it will be calendared for you.

And while we're talking about getting a grip on our schedules, be sure to plan for some just-the-two-of-you time as well. It will communicate to your children the importance you give to investing in marriage. Cindy and I make sure we have a date night every week, a special time together or away every month, and a time away together every year.

Let's pray together:

> *Holy Spirit of the living God,*
> *Awaken me! Arouse me and stir me up to action. I ask*
> *that You would ignite the souls of my children! I can only*
> *love because You have first loved me. Make me hungry to*
> *feast on Your love in a real and authentic way. Humble*
> *me as I parent my children, constantly reminding me that*
> *I am Your child and that You are parenting me. Give me*
> *the grace to see difficult times with my kids as Your gentle*
> *hand of reproof and discipline in my personal life. With*

*open hands, I release each of my children to You. I ask that when they go astray that they would quickly experience the consequences, that they would come to their senses, that I would be patient and love them unconditionally, and that one day we will all feast together again at Your table of love. Amen.*

## A HEART CHECKUP: PARENTAL LOVE

Great parenting begins when we humble ourselves before God and wholeheartedly embrace the truth that we are first and foremost children of God and that He is parenting us just like we want to parent our kids.

- Get alone with the Lord somewhere. Find someplace quiet where you will be interrupted. Shut off the phone. Just rest for a few minutes.
- Unload anything that's on your mind. Just give it to Him to hold while the two of you talk about other things.
- Feast on 1 John 3. Savor every phrase and digest every word. Pick out three or four of the most powerful truths that are speaking to you right where you are right now.
- Vividly imagine these truths. For example, when John says, "All who have this hope in him purify themselves, just as he is pure," you might imagine the resurrected Christ standing before you, radiating His pure glory.

Then look at yourself, and imagine that same fearful look of glory all over you.

- Pick out one thing that you believe God is calling you to do in light of all these truths. Submit them to Him, confessing your complete dependence on the power of His Spirit in your spirit to do what it is He wants you to do.
- Now, do some serious loving on your kids.
- Prepare a really special dinner as a celebration of them— not because it's their birthday or because they've done anything, but just because. The goal is to commit a random act of unconditional love.
- Don't tell them what's going on, but go all out! Use the finest dishes—it says they are special (in fact, we did away with Styrofoam cups at our church because we want our guests to drink coffee from nice cups and feel welcome. If you want Styrofoam, go to the Moose Lodge!). Serve up some awesome food. Light candles and ask everyone to dress up a little bit before they come.
- Think about what really speaks love into the heart of your kids. Ask God for guidance: He will show you what it is and how you are supposed to give it to them.

    Do they like gifts?

    Do they like words that make them feel special?

    Do they like it when you do things for them?

    Do they like just hanging out and being together?

    Do they like hugs, scratches, and back rubs?

- Whatever it is that makes them feel loved, feed it to them there at the table. They will eat it up.
- Write out some Bible verses about God's love and promises and have them in a bowl in the center of the table. Tell your kids that you love them so much that you're going to begin to pray the truths of Scripture over them, asking for the very best blessings of God.
- Let them pick out one of the pieces of paper from the bowl. Then open your Bible to the passage and read it. Let them discuss what they think it means. Then pray that prayer over your kids while asking for God's biggest and best blessings in their lives.
- Keep that bowl in the middle of the table and have them pick a verse every time you are all together. It's a new tradition!

# CHAPTER SIX

# THE HEART OF
# PARENTING

## Chamber II: Honor

*"A son honors his father, and a slave his master. If I am a
father, where is the honor due me? If I am a master, where
is the respect due me?' says the LORD Almighty."*
—MALACHI 1:6

I have a special confidence when I'm walking tight with
God, don't you? You can feel it in your heart. You can
sense it as circumstances line up with your desires. There's
a momentum that builds when you're moving according to
biblical principles, following the moment-by-moment leading
of the Spirit.

I felt that confidence full force back when God was knitting my heart together with Cindy's. All the biblical criteria I had been looking for in a future mate she had in abundance. And it didn't hurt that she was totally hot (still is, by the way). Sparks were flying, and the Spirit was moving. I felt like I was revved up at the stoplight of godly romance, ready to peel out. Cindy was seat-belted in, ready for the ride. I had a full tank of testosterone supercharging my engine and an open road in front of the two of us. It was clearly time to get the show on the road.

Before we started rolling, however, I was looking forward to doing something that I had always dreamed of: I wanted to honor my future father-in-law by asking for permission to pursue his daughter. When I told Cindy I wanted to talk to her dad first, it endeared me to her all the more. By showing honor to her father man-to-man, I was showing honor to her as well. I know that's not the way it usually happens in our culture anymore. But I knew that honorable things are exceptional things, and I looked forward to making the gesture.

The journey was about to begin just as I had planned. Then, in an instant, it all stalled out. He said, "No." And he didn't just say, "No." He said, "No, no, no, no, no."

"I don't have a peace about this, Shannon," he told me. "Do not pursue her. Don't call her. Don't even write letters to her. If your paths cross in ministry, so be it. But nothing more."

I was stunned. It just didn't compute. I mean, come on, I had this all mapped out. I was trying to do something godly by asking him for his endorsement of my dreams. I had complete confidence that it was time to start moving in the same direction with Cindy. But then, BLAM! No! No! No! No! This guy shot out all four tires on my dreams, bringing my life to a screeching, smoking, skidding halt. Now, I was stranded in the middle of the intersection, storming around, yelling, and kicking up dirt.

I was like, *Dude, nobody is ever going to call you about your daughter again! He's just gonna go out and do it. Forget you!* Many unprintable words and thoughts were flying around in my brain, and plenty of them made it past my lips. For many nights I stared at the ceiling with my fist clenched and my jaw set.

It was decision time. I was at a crossroads. One road led to Cindy. The other led to something I knew very little about: honor. In my vast nineteen years of experience, I had assumed "honor" was a formality. It would take many months to learn that honor goes much, much deeper than that.

Dictionaries describe "honor" with words like *fairness, honesty, integrity in one's beliefs or actions.* Honor is also something that we do by showing *high respect, worth,* and *rank.* When it comes to parenting, honor is something we want for our kids. Yeah, "respect, worth, and rank" that's what we deserve, right? That's what we should demand in our homes, right?! Hmmmm. Maybe it's time to think about that. Honor really does go much, much deeper than that.

If we want to see honor in our home, we must first become accountable, for honor always begins with personal, parental responsibility.

I'm telling you, if you embrace this concept of honor, it will radically change your world. Bringing honor to the table can be a catalyst that starts a chain reaction of good in your family. When we become accountable to the timeless principles of God, when we begin to respect and follow the authorities that God has given us, *then* honor comes to the rest of our lives.

- Honor acknowledges
- Honor applauds
- Honor appreciates
- Honor encourages
- Honor services
- Honor elevates everything
- Honor compliments

Simply, everything goes better with honor. It's like mashed potatoes. I say serve it with everything: Marriage, business, school, neighborhood, church, sex, athletics, academics, you name it. Honor causes the quality of life to go up. When honor is present in relationships, we go higher relationally, socially, morally, spiritually, and economically.

Honor may not be trendy. It's way more popular to be anti-establishment. In our culture, we dishonor the honorable. We honor the dishonorable. We raise up junk and rebellion and sell the stuff that shocks because that's what people want to buy.

Everyone wants honor, but very few get it. That sure is the way it is with parenting. Without the heartbeat of honor, nothing else seems to matter. But the more we want it, the less we seem to get it. What's wrong with this picture?

## THE HEART OF HONOR

In the year 550 B.C., the nation of Israel was in a downward spiral. The economy was down. Morale was down. The cities had become bastions of debauchery (that's a nasty-sounding word, isn't it, "debauchery"?). Things were bad and going in a worse direction fast. Sound familiar? It was the twenty-first century, twenty-one centuries ago. Into this darkness, God spoke words of light through the prophet Malachi, illuminating the core of their problem:

> *"A son honors his father, and a slave his master. If I am a father, where is the honor due me? If I am a master,*

*where is the respect due me?' says the LORD Almighty.*"
—MALACHI 1:6

The problem for the Israelites was the same problem that many of us face today: God had become commonplace.

Honor elevates things that are exceptional, but they weren't doing that with God. The holy, majestic, authoritative King of kings and Lord of lords and what His Word says had become ho-hum. That's lethal. Honor puts value on something. Honor makes something exceptional. We dishonor something by treating it as usual or common, and that's what so many of us do with God today.

This is a huge problem for kids who have grown up in the church. They've been in church ever since they can remember. They've heard every sermon. They've sung every song. Their youth pastors have tried every trick in the book to snap them out of their trance. And perhaps worst of all, they don't see any fire in the lives of their parents. Yes, maybe "Jesus is in the house." Maybe everybody at one point invited Him in to have dinner. But right now, does anybody really even seem to care?

In Matthew 13:57, Jesus says, "A prophet is not without honor except in his own town and in his own home." If your parenting has lost its edge, if your family has lost its fire, take your *own* pulse first. Where is *your* honor-meter pointing? Consider a major moment that took place in the town of Bethany:

> *Here a dinner was given in Jesus' honor. Martha served, while Lazarus was among those reclining at the table with him. Then Mary took about a pint of pure nard, an expensive perfume; she poured it on Jesus' feet and wiped his feet with her hair. And the house was filled with the fragrance of the perfume. But one of his disciples, Judas Iscariot, who was later to betray him, objected, "Why wasn't this perfume sold and the money given to the poor? It was worth a year's wages." He did not say this because he cared about the poor but because he was a thief; as keeper of the money bag, he used to help himself to what was put into it.* —JOHN 12:2-6

Any question about who gave honor that night? Maybe it's time to do something exceptional, something extravagant, something so out of the ordinary that everybody at the table in your house wakes up. Honor will radically blow your mind and put your faith on the line. This is the telltale sign of true obedience for Christ-followers. It's the ticket to spiritual success. And it will radically impact everyone around you.

We need to be serious about being children of God so that we can raise up a generation of children that are passionate about God. You can't have positive, healthy relationships without honor. Ultimately, honor is found when you, as children of God, say "Yes" and submit to the Father. Where do you start?

## Honor Through Prayer

Prayer is honorable to God. I'm not just talking about reciting the Lord's Prayer at church or repeating a common blessing before every meal (though that can be a sincere part of it). Think of prayer this way: Jesus promised that He would always be with us and that He would be in us (Matthew 28:20, John 14:20). That means prayer can and should be an ongoing spiritual conversation with our awesome, ever-present Lord—a conversation that honors Him moment by moment of every day by acknowledging His exceptional presence in us, and around us, without ceasing (1 Thessalonians 5:17).

## Honor Through Giving

We also honor God with our resources . . . No, let me correct that, with *His* resources which He has entrusted to us to use for His kingdom:

> *This will bring health to your body and nourishment to your bones. Honor the* Lord *with your wealth, with the firstfruits of all your crops; then your barns will be filled to overflowing, and your vats will brim over with new wine.* —PROVERBS 3:8-10

The next time you're sitting at the table paying bills, make it worship! I helped my kids understand how much their cell phones cost by asking them to send me a verse from their daily Bible reading. No reading, no phone privileges. I reminded them of their monthly cost, and the verses started flowing again. Bring your kids into it and show them where God's resources are going. Together, ask God to bless your family's tithe. Brainstorm on worthy causes that you can invest in to bring glory to His name. He promises if we do this, we will have more than we need, so we can keep on giving more.

### Honor Through Respect

We honor God when we show respect for the leaders He has placed in our lives. Ultimately, we can't control whether our kids will respect us or not. But I'd say it's extremely unlikely that they will if we don't respect those God has commanded us to honor. "Have confidence in your leaders and submit to their authority, because they keep watch over you as those who must give an account. Do this so that their work will be a joy, not a burden, for that would be of no benefit to you." (Hebrews 13:17, NLT).

That includes politicians and government officials. Yes, even in today's highly polarized political climate. We don't have to agree with them, but we must show them honor:

> *Let everyone be subject to the governing authorities, for there is no authority except that which God has established. The authorities that exist have been established by God. Consequently, whoever rebels against the authority is rebelling against what God has instituted, and those who do so will bring judgment on themselves.* —ROMANS 13:1-2

Seriously, if our kids see us disrespecting leaders we disagree with, how can we expect them to respect us when they disagree with us? Just think about it.

We also need to teach them to be respectful in the small things. Like saying, "Please" and "Thank you." If you're at the store and hear a mom at checkout tell their kid, "Say thank you," you know that's not being taught at home. We tell our kids that they don't walk on the Joneses' grass; we use the sidewalk. Why? Because that's their property, and we respect it.

### Honor Through Humility

Honor isn't just about our actions. Honor is all about our heart. Check out another powerful moment with Jesus:

> *One Sabbath, when Jesus went to eat in the house of a prominent Pharisee, he was being carefully watched. When he noticed how the guests picked the places of honor at the table, he told them this parable: "When someone invites*

*you to a wedding feast, do not take the place of honor, for a person more distinguished than you may have been invited. If so, the host who invited both of you will come and say to you, 'Give this person your seat.' Then, humiliated, you will have to take the least important place. But when you are invited, take the lowest place, so that when your host comes, he will say to you, 'Friend, move up to a better place.' Then you will be honored in the presence of all the other guests. For all those who exalt themselves will be humbled, and those who humble themselves will be exalted."* —LUKE 14:1, 7-11

That's a straightforward verse from God's Word. Want some more? "Wisdom's instruction is to fear the Lord, and humility comes before honor" (Proverbs 13:15). "Pride brings a person low, but the lowly in spirit gain honor" (Proverbs 29:23). "Therefore the Lord, the God of Israel, declares: 'I promised that members of your family would minister before me forever.' But now the Lord declares: 'Far be it from me! Those who honor me I will honor, but those who despise me will be disdained" (1 Samuel 2:30).

I could go on and on about this. Humility and honor are the Siamese twins of the Bible. This isn't odd; this is the way the kingdom of God works. The humble are exalted. Those who first honor God are the ones that He honors. Are you getting this? We will get to the verse about "children honor your father and mother" in just a little bit, but just remember:

- We have to be great kids so that we can raise great kids.
- Honor cannot be demanded. It must be earned.
- Honor is something your kids will give you when they catch it from you.
- Honor demanded is honor denied, but honor learned will be honor earned.

You may be able to demand honor when kids are little, but by the time they start growing hair all over, you better have earned it. If you try to demand honor then that you haven't earned, it's going to be a mess.

If there's an honor problem in our home, we must check our own honor first. It's likely because we struggle in our honoring of God. That's really the bottom line.

When honor is present, I'm telling you it is sweet. A whole different atmosphere infuses the home:

> *Let the peace of Christ rule in your hearts, since as members of one body you were called to peace. And be thankful. Let the message of Christ dwell among you richly as you teach and admonish one another with all wisdom through psalms, hymns, and songs from the Spirit, singing to God*

*with gratitude in your hearts. And whatever you do,*
*whether in word or deed, do it all in the name of the Lord*
*Jesus, giving thanks to God the Father through him. Wives,*
*submit yourselves to your husbands, as is fitting in the Lord.*
*Husbands, love your wives and do not be harsh with them.*
*Children, obey your parents in everything, for this pleases*
*the Lord. Fathers, do not embitter your children, or they*
*will become discouraged.* —COLOSSIANS 3:15-21

That's about as simple a to-do list as you could ask for in godly parenting. It's also simply impossible to do unless you are trusting in Christ to do it through you. These are the kinds of things that you cannot do in your own strength. But when we depend on Him, all things are possible. Do your part first. By God's grace, you'll be opening the door and inviting your kids into an honorable life as well.

## DEMONSTRATING HONOR IN THE HOME

In Scripture, we are sometimes commanded to obey "just because." God isn't obligated to give us any sort of rationale for what He does or tells us to do. (Just ask Job!). Cindy's dad owed me no explanation for his "No." Sometimes, though, God does explain. And He takes special care to give reasons to children for honoring their parents:

> *Children . . . "Honor your father and mother"—which is*
> *the first commandment with a promise—so that it may*
> *go well with you and that you may enjoy long life on the*
> *earth.* —EPHESIANS 6:2-3

Every command of God has its benefits. The command to honor your father and mother comes with a lot of them. Here are just three:

It Provides Protection. When children place themselves under God-given leadership, that leadership creates an umbrella of safety for them.

It Accelerates Maturity. Children can't take a pill for maturity. They have to be serious about the Word of God and learning from those who have gone before them. Sure, everyone has to learn by experience, but life will go well and you'll live longer if you become teachable, learning from others!

It Gives a Heightened Sense of Uniqueness. There's a reason medals of honor are given to so few people. They are special. The uniqueness of saying "Yes" to and honoring God's word makes you a standout.

Our kids are much more likely to experience these benefits if we take the initiative to make them a reality around the table. We don't want to force our kids to honor us at the table, but we can sure set the table in a way that influences them toward a life of honor. Here are some ways to do that.

## 1) Honor Your Parents.

Honor starts in the heart and overflows into our actions. Or at least it should. I'll never forget a memorial service at our church for a very godly man. He had led a great family that I love with all my heart. He was a lover of Christ. I sometimes imagine that he's attending our services now as one of the "great cloud of witnesses" in Hebrews 13. But that day, as his sons and daughters came by the casket, one of his children leaned over into it and said something I will never forget: "Dad, I'm so sorry that I waited this long to invest in honoring you. I'm so sorry I waited this long."

They had spent thousands of dollars on a casket and flowers and a headstone and pictures to honor him in his passing, but they didn't do it while he was alive. They didn't honor him as they could have on earth.

Certainly, there's a powerful lesson there for us all: Why wait? Honor is something that we can bring to the table anytime, every time, all the time, for any reason or no reason at all. Why wait? Why not throw a special dinner for your parents for no other reason than to give them honor where they have earned it? Remember: honor acknowledges, applauds, appreciates, compliments, encourages, serves, and elevates everything that is good. Do it for your parents now, and, who knows, maybe someday your kids will do it for you too.

### 2) Honor the Leaders.

Gen X parents have started catering to their children so much that they have come to expect the seat of honor at the table. That's biblical anarchy. Honor is earned, not demanded. I say it's time to demote the kids by training them to show simple expressions of honor to their leaders:

- Parents get the ends of the table.
- Parents get the first bite.
- Kids get to do the dishes.

I'm not talking about putting kids down, just putting them in their proper place.

### 3) Honor the Provision.

Our church has done a lot of work in Haiti, but we have gained a lot from it in return. You really don't look at a full plate of food the same when you have seen a city full of people who have none. How do we increase our appreciation for the exceptional food God has supplied us in this country?

**Give thanks**. At the table during the Last Supper, Jesus took the bread, broke it, blessed it, and gave thanks. Every molecule of food on our tables is a gracious provision from our great Provider. Give Him sincere thanks before taking a bite.

**Control the menu**. Okay, this is a pet peeve: Mom puts a gorgeous meal on the table, but little Joe gets macaroni and cheese every time because that's all he likes. Well, little Joe needs to start learning how to eat broccoli, okay? Don't tell me, "Macaroni and cheese is all he'll eat." Really? Let little Joe come and stay with us for four days! When kids learn to honor and eat what you place in front of them, they are also learning to honor and eat the truth that God places in front of them, even when they don't like it.

**Serve health**. Your meals are contributing to the future health of your children both physically and spiritually. What are you putting on the table? Is it processed? Is it microwaved? Is it quick stuff? Perhaps your physical food reflects the spiritual food you're providing for your kids at your spiritual table when they come to feast from your life. When you are feasting on the Word of God and intimate times of prayer, then you have something to feed them. But if you're spiritual pantry is empty? The best you can do is offer fast-food Christianity, which makes them obese and lazy.

## 4) Honor Your Kids.

Kids desire honor just like you do. You can respect them and bring honor to your table by developing a handful of habits:

**Listen.** Make sure everyone around the table gets a chance to be heard without interruption.

**Care.** Be interested in what interests them. Learn about their friends. Talk about their favorite sports, books, bands, etc.

**Celebrate.** One of my friends has a special "celebrate plate" that the kids get to eat off when they've done something exceptional. It doesn't have to be a huge accomplishment, but a huge compliment inspires them and affirms them.

**Enjoy.** These years will not last forever. Lean back and cross your arms and savor some of those ordinary family moments with your kids.

**Chill.** It must be some kind of a common failing, because Paul addressed it specifically in Ephesians 6:1: "Fathers, do not exasperate your children; instead, bring them up in the training and instruction of the Lord."

**Pray.** I was having dinner at a friend's house, and before the meal, he made a special point to pray for his kids. I mean, he *really* prayed biblical truth over his kids, something like this:

"Lord Jesus, I want to thank you so much that my kids are the head and not the tail, the top, not the bottom, blessing coming in, and blessed going out (Deuteronomy 28:13). I thank you that my kids are fearfully and wonderfully made (Psalm 139:14). Thank you that you have chosen them" (Colossians 3:12).

Here's the deal. Proverbs 18:20 says that the power of life and the power of death are in the tongue. When you speak, you unleash the power to hurt or harm. Let your prayers coat your kids with life-giving truth.

**Believe.** Guard your thoughts about them. Proverbs 4:23 (GNT) says, "Be careful how you think; your life is shaped by your thoughts." Just because you think it doesn't make it true. So, when you are tempted to get discouraged by the way your children seem to be acting or heading, think thoughts God has promised for them.

The end result of all of this is that God gets the praise and God gets the honor when the things that He honors are honored in the home. Let there be nothing above him. Let everything be below him. "You are worthy, our Lord and God, to receive glory and honor and power, for you created all things, and by your will they were created and have their being" (Revelation 4:11).

Bottom line: We have a mission, to honor God. We have purpose, to honor God, And it's not prep time. It is go time.

## SECOND-TIME SUCCESS

It took a good long while to get my wits about me after Cindy's dad denied me permission to pursue her. A lot of prayer, a lot of long walks, and few cold showers helped. Sixteen months passed and, dare I say, a big boy became a young man during that time. I had survived the most intense disappointment and rejection of my life. In the aftermath, I had matured in a quantum leap as I wrestled with desire and denial.

As the Spirit searched my heart and showed me my ways, I learned to place my confidence in God rather than myself. I learned that my security and identity come from Christ and not a girl or any other relationship, and I made the decision to serve the Lord in full-time ministry. God had captured my attention in new ways as I probed the depths of honor and what it meant to honor those He honors.

After I turned twenty-one, my path crossed with Cindy's again. We were at a retreat center for a couple of weeks of training at the home base of a revival ministry. All the feelings and desires I had buried came back. But this time, it was different. It was different because I was different. Now, eighteen months later, I felt the confidence of walking with the Lord again, but even that was different. This time it was mixed with humility. Over the last year and a half, honor had taken me deeper than I had ever gone before.

After several days of focused prayer, I knew it was time to honor Cindy's father one more time. This time, it was no formality. No cockiness, no assumptions; this was real. I was pursuing a relationship with Cindy's father so that I could pursue an earthly bride. But the Spirit was really asking me to pursue my heavenly Father to develop His ministry and develop His bride.

Not at all certain of what the answer would be, I picked up the phone and dialed. This time, Cindy's father said, "Yes. Shannon, I sense and discern what God has done in your life. I'm very much ready to give you permission to pursue my daughter."

The next thing I knew, I was sitting across the table from Cindy at that Olive Garden, babbling like a giddy kid. Ten months later, I was at another table in a restaurant south of Memphis, weeping as Cindy's father and mother gave me their blessing to marry their daughter.

That's just about everything that I know about honor and what it means for children to honor parents and, ultimately, honor God. Oh, and I do know one other thing: If some punk nineteen-year-old kid comes asking about my daughter, he better be ready.

Let's pray:

> *Holy Father,*
> *You are worthy, my Lord and God, to receive glory and*
> *honor and power. You created all things. By Your will they*
> *were created and have their being. I sincerely ask, in the*
> *name of Jesus and by the power of Your Holy Spirit in me,*
> *that You would be honored in my home, and that my kids*
> *may experience that honor and choose to honor You in all*
> *that they do.*
> *Amen.*

## A HEART CHECKUP: HONOR

- Read and ponder Colossians 3:1-21. What parts of this passage seem to be speaking to you the loudest?
- Pour out your heart to the Lord and declare your dependence on Christ and the presence of the Holy Spirit in you to make this happen.
- Review the section about the ways we, as individuals, can honor God. Then:
- *Pray.* Communicate openly and continually with Christ, honoring His presence as radically exceptional.
- *Give.* Ask the Holy Spirit to show you the specific ways He wants you to give God's resources in order to bring Him honor. Be open to Him leading you in unique ways.

- *Respect.* Consider all the leaders God has placed over you. How can you tangibly show God honor by honoring them?
- *Humility.* Read Matthew 14. What does God seem to be showing you about yourself in this parable?

## REFLECTING A HEART OF HONOR IN YOUR HOME

- Read John 12:1-19 as a family, with each person reading one verse at a time.
- Identify all the main characters in the passage.
- Assign someone to be the narrator, then someone to do each of the different voices.
- Re-read it as dramatically as possible.
- Which characters wanted to make Jesus "common"? Which characters wanted to honor Jesus by doing something exceptional?
- Which character are you most like?
- Brainstorm some crazy things you could do to bring Jesus honor as a family.

# CHAPTER SEVEN

# THE HEART OF PARENTING

## Chamber III: Training

> *"He is wooing you from the jaws of distress to a spacious place free from restriction, to the comfort of your table laden with choice food."*
> —JOB 36:16

**W**hen it comes to priorities in training our kids, I think most of us are only about 180 degrees off. We're close—except that everything on the top of the list should be on the bottom, and everything on the bottom should probably be on the top. Other than that, I think we're doing pretty well!

Sarcasm aside, take an honest look at what we prioritize: education, sports, and entertainment. There's nothing wrong with any of those things. In fact, God endorses them all at different places in the scriptures. And let's face it; we love it when our kids excel in these areas because it really makes us look good in public. But God is far more concerned about what's happening in the privacy of our own hearts. Do our priorities match His?

*"Do not store up for yourselves treasures on earth, where moths and vermin destroy, and where thieves break in and steal. But store up for yourselves treasures in heaven, where moths and vermin do not destroy, and where thieves do not break in and steal. For where your treasure is, there your heart will be also . . . No one can serve two masters. Either you will hate the one and love the other, or you will be devoted to the one and despise the other. You cannot serve both God and money . . . So do not worry, saying, 'What shall we eat?' or 'What shall we drink?' or 'What shall we wear?' For the pagans run after all these things, and your heavenly Father knows that you need them. But seek first his kingdom and his righteousness, and all these things will be given to you as well."* —MATTHEW 6:19-21, 24, 31-33

Honestly, aren't the vast majority of the stressors in our life because we have our priorities screwed up? We're *so* focused on the things that are not that important. We spend our money and time and passions running here and there trying to get this and that and provide our kids with everything that they need to be "successful." We're going so fast that we rarely rest, rarely refocus on the things that have never-ending value and honor. When Job's life was so messed up, Elihu, one of his buddies, had the wisdom to help him put things in perspective:

> *"Bear with me a little longer and I will show you that there is more to be said in God's behalf. I get my knowledge from afar; I will ascribe justice to my Maker. Be assured that my words are not false; one who has perfect knowledge is with you . . . He is wooing you from the jaws of distress to a spacious place free from restriction to the comfort of your table laden with choice food."* —JOB 36:2-4, 16

In the midst of all Job's illness, death, bankruptcy, and pain, Elihu told him that God was gently releasing him from all the things that had consumed his attention. God was inviting Job to intimacy with Him, just like Jesus did for us.

Put yourself in Job's shoes for a moment. (Well, actually, at this point, he didn't even have any shoes. Just a bunch of festering boils on his skin, but you know what I mean.) Imagine all of the things that are bringing distress to you right now. Can you list them? Now, feel the gentle touch of a friend on your cheek as he tells you God is wooing you away from that and inviting you to draw closer to Him. Because that's what God is doing right now. He is gently calling all of us to get our priorities straight and to focus our lives first on the things that matter the most, and that bring us true life. A different version of that same passage words Job 36:16 (MSG) like this: "Oh, Job, don't you see how God's wooing you from the jaws of danger? How he's drawing you into wide-open places—inviting you to feast at a table laden with blessings?"

If you get that picture in your mind, it will truly be unforgettable. Not only that, but we have the incredible opportunity to parent in a way that trains our kids to forget about the things that don't matter and to seek first that which is unforgettable: God's kingdom.

It's all about priorities. Christ is first, irrefutably. For me, personally, this is a constant hurdle. Keeping my priorities straight as a parent was a minute-by-minute, day-by-day process of reminding myself, through the leadership of the Holy Spirit, that I was influencing my children to be world changers.

We are making disciples. You should see it that way too. God has given you a piece of history. Kids are "history in the making." Our kids will shape history for good or bad, and God has entrusted their training to us. This is why this heart chamber of training in parenting is so vital, so indispensable:

God, in His sovereign grace, has entrusted us with kids, divine pieces of history, that we are to train to make a difference that will count for eternity.

But . . . I know what you may be feeling right now. I really do, because I felt it too. Whenever I see this challenge in Scripture, my immediate response is one of intimidation. How in the world can I do that when I don't do it myself and when I fall short so often? I'm just going to punt to the Sunday school teacher, or student pastor. I'm just going to pray for the best . . .

Listen, if you're feeling inadequate to train your kids, you are absolutely right. You can't do it. In fact, you weren't designed to do it. You're incompetent! And that's the way God planned it: "Such confidence we have through Christ before God. Not that we are competent in ourselves to claim anything for ourselves, but our competence comes from God. He has made us competent as ministers of a new covenant" (2 Corinthians 3:4-6).

If you're daunted by the challenge of parenting, just echo the prayer of Manoah. He and his wife had been unable to conceive, but then an angel of the Lord appeared to her and said that God was going to give them a child. The angel had special instructions for the child, because he said the child (Samson) would grow up to deliver the Israelites from the hands of their oppressors.

What was Manoah's prayer when he learned about all this? "Pardon your servant, Lord. I beg you to let the man of God you sent to us come again to teach us how to bring up the boy who is to be born" (Judges 13:8).

As Manoah recognizes, training your kids starts with this confession: Lord, I can't do this, but You can. And You live in me. My life is Your life. I'm trusting You to do it through me.

That's where training begins, and that's where training ends, too: Trusting in the Lord rather than your own strength and abilities. God designed the Christian life to be lived this way to guarantee that the glory for anything good that happens goes to Him. The idea that God only chooses and uses people who have their act together is a lie from Satan. Check out this encounter with Jesus, and you'll see:

> *Jesus went out and saw a tax collector by the name of Levi sitting at his tax booth. "Follow me," Jesus said to him, and Levi got up, left everything and followed him. Then Levi held a great banquet for Jesus at his house, and a large crowd of tax collectors and others were eating with them. But the Pharisees and the teachers of the law who belonged to their sect complained to his disciples, "Why do you eat and drink with tax collectors and sinners?" Jesus answered them, "It is not the healthy who need a doctor,*

> *but the sick. I have not come to call the righteous, but sin-*
> *ners to repentance."* —LUKE 5:27-32

Seriously, if you look at the people that Jesus hung out with, there was really only one requirement: you had to be really messed up. Jesus hung out with messes, and our kids need to know that. We need to remember that. Jesus didn't come to dine with healthy people; He came to dine with the sick ones who knew they couldn't do it on their own.

Don't think for a second that I always had my act together at my house. It regularly had the rumblings of an earthquake. We battled huge issues—crazy issues that you wouldn't think a pastor is supposed to deal with. There were so many things that I needed to change in my approach to parenting. When I think about "training," I have to look back and ask, "What does this look like in my own life? Am I submitting as a kid so that my kids submit?"

I encourage you, as Christ-followers, to be transparent about these things. It's time to take off our masks and quit pretending that we have it all together. *Nobody* does. You can try to fake it in your own strength, but the Christian life really boils down to this: the grace of God and the power of His Spirit living through us.

If you're a child of God, you must realize that you're a piece of history as God's child as well. He's not done with you. You're not here just to be saved and then be done. You're here to shape God's plan. God is sovereign; it's up to Him, but He wants to use you. His Spirit is in you, and He has chosen to use you to make the difference. He wants to shape you to shape your kids in a way that allows their lives to change eternity through His power. There is no limit on what God can do through you as His child. The only limit is the one you put on God. So don't limit Him. *Trust* Him.

Let's start with just a couple of irrefutable training principles:

### 1) Lead Intentionally.

Training will not happen unless you are intent on making it happen. It's highly unlikely that your children will figure all this out on their own. I have seen rare exceptions where God raises a child up out of a very dark, difficult, sinful situation. But most of the time, kids are trained because the parent is intentionally setting priorities, training, and leading in the home.

### 2) Lead with Initiative.

What do you want to do? What do you want be? What do you want to see happen? God is ready to use you to do these things; you just must humbly submit and then step out in strategic faith to see it happen.

### 3) Lead Indirectly.

Kids are more likely to be trained by what you do rather than what you say. There's that saying that things are caught, not taught. It's called modeling. Ephesians 5:1 (ESV) says, "... be imitators of God." 1 Corinthians 11:1 says, "Follow my example, as I follow the example of Christ."

For example, we want to train our kids to be part of a vibrant community of believers on a regular basis. Statistics tell us that if both mom and dad take their kids to church, 72% of them will attend church as adults. If Dad takes the kids to church, 55% of them will go to church as adults. But if Mom is the only one going to church with their child, only 15% of those kids will attend as adults. (Think about that, dads!) If Mom and Dad are CEO attendees (CEO stands for "Christmas and Easter, Only"), 86% of their kids will never attend church after turning eighteen.

### 4) Lead Immediately.

You might think it's too late. Maybe your kid is already a legal adult. But yesterday is history and tomorrow never comes. Today is all you've got. All I can say is that don't let arbitrary American numbers influence your training. There's nothing magical about turning eighteen in God's kingdom. What are we supposed to say? "Happy birthday to you! God bless you! I'm done with you!"

I think eighteen is a great age by which to get them on their feet, be responsible, have vocational focus and vision, and all those things. But you still have influence. After they "leave and cleave," you're wise if you don't get in their business, but you can still lead indirectly by modeling. It's going to be more "show" than "tell" at this point. (Unless they ask you for advice, I'd give it very, very sparingly.) Your children will always be observing you as a child of God and learning from your example.

It should go without saying that leading means taking responsibility. But many parents these days seem reluctant to be firm. They just want to be best buddies with their kids. That's not our role! Yes, we can have a great relationship with them, but our job is to disciple them in the ways of Jesus. That means saying "No" sometimes.

If these are some principles for leading our kids, how can we start to put them into practice? By turning to the best book in the universe to tell us the next steps.

## THE GUIDEBOOK IN THE GOOD BOOK

God's Word is the beginning and the end of all godly training. That book has proven itself over and over again to be living, active, and authoritative in all aspects of life. Not only that, but tucked right in the middle of the Bible is a book that was written specifically to help train kids.

Solomon was the son of King David. He was arguably the wealthiest and wisest man that has ever lived. In the prime of his life, he wrote the book of Proverbs—thirty-one chapters full of pointed, powerful, practical wisdom. He wrote it to his kids, and now it has been passed down so that we can share it with our kids.

Proverbs 22:6 (KJV) says, "Train up a child in the way he should go: and when he is old, he will not depart from it." The word train in the original Hebrew means "to dedicate" and "to initiate." That's so powerful, because that's exactly what God does with each of us as His children. His spirit in us draws us into a dedicated relationship with God, where He continually initiates us into His ways as He draws us to Himself and into daily repentance.

The Proverbs are loaded with training material about the most practical and important aspects of life. Here are just seven points that I feel are especially important:

**Number 1: Train them to select their friends carefully.**
You want to make sure your kids' best friends are quality individuals that are shaping their future. I'm not saying you don't want to encourage them to reach out to the lost and those that are hurting. But make sure that your children are the influencers, not the influenced.

When one of our kids wanted to spend the night at the house of a friend we weren't sure about, we didn't just say no. Instead, we'd offer to have the sleepover at our house. And we'd just involve their friends in the routines of our home: prayer at mealtimes, prayers before bed. Those guests were invited along to church with us, too, and some came to faith in Christ and were baptized.

Proverbs 13:20-21 says, "Walk with the wise and become wise, for a companion of fools suffers harm. Trouble pursues the sinner, but the righteous are rewarded with good things."

**Number 2: Train them on how to manage God's money.**
The book of Proverbs is jam-packed with tons of excellent training about how we should view money, get money, save money, and give money.

"Honor the LORD with your wealth, with the first fruits of all your crops;

then your barns will be filled to overflowing, and your vats will brim over with new wine" (Proverbs 3:9-10). "Do not wear yourself out to get rich; do not trust your own cleverness.

Cast but a glance at riches, and they are gone, for they will surely sprout wings and fly off to the sky like an eagle" (Proverbs 23:4-5).

**Number 3: Train them to watch their words.**
Don't let your kids just say anything they want. Words are powerful. Show them the power of their words by modeling encouragement and speaking the truth. And I say it's time to dump the double standard some of us have. The Bible says that some words are "unwholesome." If your kids shouldn't say certain words, you shouldn't say them either.

Proverbs has a lot to say about this. "Keep your mouth free of perversity; keep corrupt talk far from your lips" (Proverbs 4:24). "Whoever conceals hatred with lying lips and spreads slander is a fool. Sin is not ended by multiplying words, but the prudent hold their tongues. The tongue of the righteous is choice silver but the heart of the wicked is of little value" (Proverbs 10:18-20).

When we went on vacation when our kids were small, we couldn't afford to fly. That meant long hours driving together, with the potential for some backseat fighting. I made T-shirts for them to wear that read "No Negs," and told them there was to be no negativity: we would only speak honorably to each other.

**Number 4: Train them to be responsible.**
Proverbs 6:6-8 says, "Go to the ant, you sluggard; consider its ways and be wise! It has no commander, no overseer or

ruler, yet it stores its provisions in summer and gathers its food at harvest."

Sadly, I'm afraid we have lost most of a generation of hard workers. Yes, there are a few Gen Xers who are working hard, but many have lotion hands. We just think if we go to college, we've got it made. Not anymore. You can go to college, and you can get all the degrees you want, and still end up not being able to afford to have the heat on where you live. You must have a good attitude, and you must have a work ethic. I don't care where you graduated from; I want to know if you can work. Unfortunately, we have taught people that schoolwork rather than hard work gets you paid excellently. That's wrong, and it's unbiblical.

The Bible says, "children are a blessing." Well, you know what they are blessed to do? Clean their rooms, wash the dishes, mow the lawn, and buy your meal once in a while.

### Number 5: Train them to guard their hearts.
"Above all else, guard your heart, for everything you do flows from it" (Proverbs 4:23).

A child's heart and mind are extremely valuable and extremely vulnerable. Train your children to protect them. Don't just allow anything to come into their minds. Filter what they read and what they watch on television. Make sure any device with internet access can only be viewed through passwords in a non-private part of the house. Broken bones and bruises will heal themselves. But when a kid's heart and mind take a hit, the damage will probably stay with them forever in one way or another. So teach them to protect their own hearts and minds.

With that in mind, let me encourage you to be careful about how much access they have to the internet. We required our kids to place their phones outside their rooms, in the hallway, at 9:00 p.m. They didn't need to be texting with who knows who and surfing who knows where late into the night. Letting kids have a phone with no limits is like handing them a stick of dynamite, lighting the fuse, and wishing them well.

**Number 6: Train them to be generous.**
"One person gives freely, yet gains even more; another withholds unduly, but comes to poverty. A generous person will prosper; whoever refreshes others will be refreshed" (Proverbs 11:24-25).

Most kids' first word is "Mama." A close second often is "Mine!" Sound familiar? It does to me because, to be honest, it sounds a lot like me. Most of us were never really trained that nothing is "mine" and that everything is God's. But it is.

Everything that we have is just on temporary loan, to be used for His honor and glory.

Like almost everything else we've discussed in this book, generosity can be taught, but it's better to be caught. If you want your kids to get it, just get into it yourself and bring them along for the ride. For years, we had the tradition of going to eat at Waffle House on Christmas Eve. Stylish dining, right? But we didn't go there for what's on the menu. We went for who was waiting on the tables.

See, I figured that if you're working the Christmas Eve shift at Waffle House, you must really need the money, and you mustn't be afraid of hard work. So, we would go, eat, and leave as generous a tip as we could—at least a couple hundred dollars in cash. When the wait staff said thank you, I would just explain that Jesus had changed my life, and He had called us to share His good news with everyone else.

I knew this practice had hit home when, after one such Christmas Eve visit, one of my children said on the way home, "Dad, now I know why we drive a '99 suburban."

Generous giving is a blast. Discovering where God wants you to give next is part of the adventure. It builds faith in God's provision. It builds ownership in the kingdom. And you know what? It's not all about you. It really does matter to the people on the receiving end.

**Number 7: Train them to fear God.**

Hopefully, you know by now that I'm not talking about making God out to be some sort of black cloud of impending punishment, ready to strike with His lightning bolts every time your kid steps on or over the line. No, I'm not talking about scaring them with God. We're talking about living in vibrant awareness of all the attributes of God—truths that should leave us in "awe"—because that's what the word fear means.

In the biblical context of Almighty God, that's what parental training and the book of Proverbs are all about. From cradle to graduation, we have only 216 months to have these table moments as the prioritized caregivers, so let's do this right and make it irrefutable.

I heard of one church that emphasizes to parents just how short this time of influence is in a memorable way. At their child's dedication, the parents are given a jar containing 936 small stones—one for each weekend between the child's birth and eighteenth birthday. As Mom and Dad remove a stone each, they are reminded how their days of training and nurturing are reducing.

Let's not miss any opportunity to tell and remind our kids how God's Word is their light:

> *For gaining wisdom and instruction; for understanding words of insight; for receiving instruction in prudent behavior, doing what is right and just and fair; for giving prudence to those who are simple, knowledge and discretion to the young—let the wise listen and add to their learning, and let the discerning get guidance—for understanding proverbs and parables, the sayings and riddles of the wise. The fear of the LORD is the beginning of knowledge, but fools despise wisdom and instruction.* —PROVERBS 1:2-7

### Number 8: Train them to Go.

"Train up a child in the way he should go" (Proverbs 22:6, NKJV).

Give your kid a vision to leave and live out their passion and purpose for life. I know the economy is tough, and times are challenging, but having your grown kids living rent-free in your basement at twenty-five is not cool. Getting to gold level on Xbox is not something to aspire to as a life goal. We need to be preparing them to take responsibility for their own lives from an early age. When it's time to go shopping, make sure they have worked as hard for their shoes as you have yours. If you have kids living at home when they are thirty-something, move out and ask them to take over the mortgage.

Of course, you don't quit being a parent when your kids are grown and move out, but the nature of the relationship changes. I believe that our kids still come to us for advice now they are out on their own, from time to time, because of the way we prayed with and for them when they were young.

Let's pray:

> *Oh Lord,*
> *Train me to train my kids now. I'm trusting in You to do this through me, for I am inadequate without You. With You, however, I truly believe that all things are possible. Give me the willingness to step out in faith. Make my life a model to my kids so that when they see me, they see You working through me. Guide us in Your Word for ultimate truth and instruction.*
> *Amen.*

## A HEART CHECKUP: TRAINING

- Start out by spending a little time thanking God for the truth in these passages:
  - 1 John 1:8-10—all of us are "messed up" by sin. When we admit that to God, He forgives us and cleanses us.
  - Romans 8:1—No one who is in Christ Jesus is condemned by God.

- - John 15:5—We can't do anything good without Christ doing it through us.
  - Philippians 4:13—All things can be done through the strength of Christ.
- Now read Matthew 6:24-34. Let the Holy Spirit of God really test your heart.
- What are your main worries?
- How would your life be different if you completely trusted God with these concerns?
- If you really believed that God will take care of tomorrow, how would it change your actions today?
- Prayerfully contemplate what it would mean to you if you were to "seek first the kingdom of God and his righteousness."
- Talk to Jesus about these things. Be transparent and totally honest with Him. He knows you and He loves you, and He wants to train you in new ways.

## TIME FOR TRAINING

Proverbs comes in thirty-one chapters. That's one for every day of the month, with an extra or two thrown in every once in a while. Coincidence? Maybe, but it is a convenient reason to transform your dining room into a full-blown spiritual classroom every day of the month.

Since the coronavirus pandemic shut things down, we have all gotten used to distance learning. But the best instruction still happens face to face—often at the dining table, with mouths full of food. There's no better time to talk about the things of God than when you're sharing a meal: "He humbled you, causing you to hunger and then feeding you with manna, which neither you nor your ancestors had known, to teach you that man does not live on bread alone but on every word that comes from the mouth of the LORD" (Deuteronomy 8:3).

Let's keep the no-talking-with-your-mouth-full rule in place; it provides an opportunity for everyone to learn to listen well. In addition to that, I would also encourage and enforce a no-cell-phone rule while you're eating together. Incessant texting, nonstop tweets, news checking, and flinching every time Facebook updates should be banned. Children shouldn't be allowed to have their cell phones at the table, either. Table time is sacred time.

Get a Bible for every person that's going to be at the table; just buy a few of the inexpensive ones that you can keep around for a while.

After a meal, read the chapter of Proverbs that corresponds to the day of the month. Have everyone read it silently to themselves.

Each person at the table then gets a chance to pick out the specific passage that they feel is most important for the family at that given moment.

Probe the passage with good open-ended questions:

- Why did they pick out that one passage out of all the possible passages?
- What do you think motivated Solomon to write it?
- Is the passage as relevant today as it would have been three thousand years ago, when it was written?
- What are some possible ways to specifically apply the principles in this passage?
- What could you do as a family and as individuals to make it a reality?

# CHAPTER EIGHT

# THE HEART OF PARENTING

## Chamber IV: Truth

*He humbled you, causing you to hunger and then feeding you with manna, which neither you nor your ancestors had known, to teach you that man does not live on bread alone but on every word that comes from the mouth of the LORD.*
—DEUTERONOMY 8:3

**A**healthy family is a lot like a healthy corporation. As the dad of the family, I saw myself as the CEO, the Chief Executive Officer. I was responsible for everything that happened; I was where the buck stopped, and I needed to be the one taking the primary lead when it came to vision.

Cindy was definitely the COO, the Chief Operations Officer. Without her, the whole thing would have blown apart and gone up in flames in a matter of minutes. We worked together to fulfill the role of CFO, Chief Financial Officer. But I always remembered that our kids had a stake in the corporation too.

As CEO, it was my job to protect, defend, and direct our little corporation, and I took a lot of pride in that job, actually. When I realized what I had allowed to happen in my home, I have to admit that I was embarrassed at first. Then I felt a real sense of loss. And then I got pretty mad for letting it happen under my watch. Finally, I decided to do something about it: I called a board meeting of everybody who had stock in our tribe: I guess you could have called it a "family shareholders meeting."

First, I sent out an official announcement (whistled down the hall), gathered everyone around the conference table (actually, the coffee table in the living room), and called the meeting to order. I started by sharing a lot of the awesome stuff that I saw happening in our home. (It's a good idea to affirm the positive before you have to confront the negative.) And then, I took full responsibility for the problem: I had allowed Satan to deceptively detour our family from our primary purpose. We were settling for what was temporarily good but had lost sight of what was eternally essential.

The problem is so obvious to me now, but I was blind to it. It's crazy, really, that I didn't see it. Here's the deal:

As parents, we'll sign our kids up without asking them for ball, sign 'em up for cheer, sign 'em up for dance, and sign 'em up for this and that. We make them go to school. We make them practice their instrument. We tell them that they need to be committed to their team. We say, "Get your homework done!" And we make them open their history, their algebra, their trigonometry, their biology, their English . . .

Now, there's nothing wrong with any of those things. My kids were involved in all of them, and I made them study as they should. That was all well and good. But what I had done, as CEO, was allow the "earthly good" to take priority over the "eternally essential." Cindy and I had focused our parenting on love, honor, and training—all of which were good—but we had neglected the importance of truth. Decision by decision, we had encouraged—and even trained—our kids to put their textbooks on *top* of their Bibles and their academics *before* their faith. We made sure that they learned their facts and formulas, but because our family was just as busy as yours, our kids were not getting through their pile of textbooks to the Bible at all. They made all their ball practices, but maybe only a handful of student services.

I had let the Word of God, His living truth, get buried under a bunch of academic stuff. There's really no excuse for that, but if it's any consolation, the Scriptures themselves showed me that I wasn't alone ...

Back 2500 years ago, the walls of the holy city of Jerusalem were in shambles. God called Nehemiah to right this wrong. It's an incredible story of determination, faithfulness, and sacrifice. Yet, in the process, they seem to have let their busyness get the best of them. In the midst of all their work, the word of God had gotten buried. So Nehemiah called his own shareholders' meeting:

> *All the people came together as one in the square before the Water Gate. They told Ezra the teacher of the Law to bring out the Book of the Law of Moses, which the LORD had commanded for Israel ... He read it aloud from daybreak till noon as he faced the square before the Water Gate in the presence of the men, women and others who could understand. And all the people listened attentively to the Book of the Law. Ezra the teacher of the Law stood on a high wooden platform built for the occasion ... Ezra praised the Lord, the great God; and all the people lifted their hands and responded, "Amen! Amen!" Then they bowed down and worshiped the Lord with their faces to the ground ... They read from the Book of the Law of God, making it clear and giving the meaning so that the people understood what was being read ... For all the people had been weeping as they listened to the words of*

*the Law. Nehemiah said, "Go and enjoy choice food and sweet drinks, and send some to those who have nothing prepared. This day is holy to our Lord. Do not grieve, for the joy of the Lord is your strength." The Levites calmed all the people, saying, "Be still, for this is a holy day. Do not grieve." Then all the people went away to eat and drink, to send portions of food and to celebrate with great joy, because they now understood the words that had been made known to them.* —NEHEMIAH 8:1, 3-4, 6, 8–12

I was grieved when I read that to realize that I, too, had neglected the word of God. We were concerned about our kids' physical health, and we tried to make sure they had a good diet, but we were falling short when it came to serving them Jesus as the living water and the bread of life. Yet the truth of Scripture is the most essential food group for life. By the guidance of the Spirit in them, our kids are capable of ingesting its eternal transforming truths. But they can't feast on God's Word unless it's served. That's the best thing that we can offer our kids, no matter how busy we are.

## LOSING OUR WAY AND FINDING IT AGAIN

There's really no excuse for letting the word of God get buried in our lives. But there are certain mentalities that have made it easier for us to justify letting it happen.

**Drive-through distraction.**
Good churches serve the Word of God to their people with excellence. Sometimes, though, that can become an excuse for us not feeding ourselves or our families. Just drive in and out once a week and call it good, right?

**TV-tray temptation.**
Some parents set their kids in front of Christian entertainment, hoping it will provide enough spiritual nourishment on its own. The strategy is to push the kid into youth group, or camps, or concerts with high entertainment value, hoping that somewhere along the way, they might take a bite of the truth as well. Now, that's good as far as it goes, but it's the Christian version of a television dinner. Don't stop encouraging those things, but remember that they are only the accent to what you should be feeding in your home.

**Potluck presumption.**
Everyone-bring-a-dish gatherings are awesome—once in a while. I love getting together with friends to sample the stuff they've brought. But you can't rely on other people to supply all your kids need. If that's the only way you eat, you'll never learn to serve a balanced meal on your own. The same goes with our intake of scriptural truth. If we only eat what other

people bring to the table, we might never discover how to feed ourselves what we truly need.

### Half-chewed hopefulness.

Back in the day, a late-night weekend comedy show did a skit called "Pre-Chewed Charlie's"—an advertisement for a restaurant for people that didn't like to chew their own steak. You guessed it: the waiters chewed it for them. Funny and disgusting. Unfortunately, that's how many of us get our regular intake of the Word of God. Some depend far too much on preachers and teachers to chew up and digest the word of God for them, hoping that is enough, rather than feasting on the pure words themselves.

### Bar-bouncing barrier.

I remember back when bars and bar stools were the cool thing in homes. They were convenient, for sure, but when you sat at the bar, you didn't get to talk to anybody face-to-face or look them in the eye. Some of us do the same thing with God in our study of the Scriptures. We don't want to look across into His eyes. We don't want to be honest about what we do and how we serve, and being committed to the faithful call of God to build His church, to give, to tithe, to serve, to obey. We don't want to really get that involved or committed to God, so we adopt this bar-side mentality and sit beside him instead of across from

Him. Interestingly, I don't see any bars in the Bible, and there's no bar in heaven. There's just a table—and the table is designed for connection, intimacy, and feasting.

The Bible offers a full-blown smorgasbord of truth and wisdom for life. It's like a huge buffet, lined with the very best of the very best of spiritual nourishment. There's meat and potatoes with salads galore topped off with refreshing drinks and sweet desserts. It's all edible. It's all beneficial. It's all profitable for teaching and for training and for correction and for reproof. Whether you are a spiritual infant, or think that you are mature and wise, the Bible has just what you need at every age:

> *Therefore, rid yourselves of all malice and all deceit, hypocrisy, envy, and slander of every kind. Like newborn babies, crave pure spiritual milk, so that by it you may grow up in your salvation, now that you have tasted that the Lord is good.* —1 PETER 2:1-3

> *We have much to say about this, but it is hard to make it clear to you because you no longer try to understand. In fact, though by this time you ought to be teachers, you need someone to teach you the elementary truths of God's word all over again. You need milk, not solid food! Anyone who lives on milk, being still an infant, is not acquainted with the teaching about righteousness. But solid food is for the*

*mature, who by constant use have trained themselves to
distinguish good from evil.* —HEBREWS 5:11-14

The Bible is your fuel. It's your nourishment. Don't be thinking
that you're passionate about God without being passionate
about the Bible. Sooner or later (and I'm voting for sooner),
you need to take a bite on your own or starve. If you chew it up,
the nourishment of the truth will start surging in your veins.

There's nothing complicated here. You sit down with God's Word
and open it. Then read it. It doesn't take a PhD. If you're just
starting out, I would suggest that you first read the book of James.
Then I would read plenty of Proverbs. Next, I would suggest
Paul's letter to the Ephesians. Then read some of David's Psalms.

You might want to jump right into a Bible-reading plan
designed by someone else (there are several suggestions at the
end of this chapter). The key is getting that alone time with
Jesus and the Holy Spirit with the living Word. Forget being
"too busy" and go for the best. Make the time and do it!

Once you're there, start off sincerely asking God to bless your
time and teach you what He wants you to learn. Then, all you
have to do is read and ask some key questions:

- What does it say?
- What does it mean?

- How does it relate to me?
- What do I do about it?

Under the guidance and power of the Spirit, you honor the Word of God by honoring the things that the Word of God reveals. The nice thing is that you can do all of this immediately with your children. You don't have to have all the answers. You just have to know the questions!

Start with John's Gospel, perhaps. Make some time to be with your kids and just start asking the same questions with them that you ask yourself. Your kids will think you're brilliant! They will think you are the famous Greek philosopher Socrates. (Everybody thought he was so smart, but all he really did was sit around and ask people questions all day. That guy had it made.)

If your kids start asking questions and they stick you for an answer that you don't know, just utter six magic words: "I don't know. I'll find out." Then call your pastor. (That's why you pay him the big bucks!)

I know this may sound a little intimidating if you've never done it before. But there's something powerful about honoring God's Word with the people that God wants you to honor. We're not just supposed to be fed. God wants us to be feeders *while* we are being fed. We do this by sharing the feast with

others and modeling how they can invite others to the table
and share the feast with them too. Paul worded it this way:

> *You then, my son, be strong in the grace that is in Christ
> Jesus. And the things you have heard me say in the presence
> of many witnesses entrust to reliable people who will also
> be qualified to teach others.* —2 TIMOTHY 2:1-2

This is huge! God can use you as the first link in a new "spiritual
food chain" that will nourish your family with the truth, and
then their families, and their families for generations to come.
That was the vision behind the command that God gave to
the people of Israel:

> *These are the commands, decrees and laws the LORD your
> God directed me to teach you to observe in the land that you
> are crossing the Jordan to possess, so that you, your children
> and their children after them may fear the LORD your God
> as long as you live by keeping all his decrees and commands
> that I give you, and so that you may enjoy long life. Hear,
> Israel, and be careful to obey so that it may go well with
> you and that you may increase greatly in a land flowing
> with milk and honey, just as the LORD, the God of your
> ancestors, promised you. Hear, O Israel: The LORD our God,
> the LORD is one. Love the LORD your God with all your
> heart and with all your soul and with all your strength.
> These commandments that I give you today are to be on*

*your hearts. Impress them on your children. Talk about them when you sit at home and when you walk along the road, when you lie down and when you get up. Tie them as symbols on your hands and bind them on your foreheads. Write them on the doorframes of your houses and on your gates.* —DEUTERONOMY 6:1-9

When I was little, my mom took passages like this to heart. She didn't write on our doorframes, exactly, though I know some people do. What she did was pin a little Scripture-related 5x7 postcard on a corkboard by the breakfast bar in our house. It was a picture of the rapture that had been popular back in the 70s. Pretty horrifying for a little kid, actually: Planes were crashing into buildings; people were getting resurrected and ascending out of tombs; taxis were smashing into each other. Fuel for nightmares, for sure. I remember leaning over and looking at that thing while Mom was stirring something at the stove.

"Mom," I asked, "if Jesus comes back, will I be going to heaven?" What followed was one of the most important moments of my life. Mom sat down with me and shared from the Scriptures what it meant to be a Christian and to go to heaven. That was a long time ago, but I remember it all as clearly as anything. My mom understood that she could take the lead in bringing the Scriptures into our home.

That passage in Deuteronomy is talking about a home that is saturated with the Word of God. There's no drive-through, no television tray, potluck, pre-chewed, bar-bouncing mentality in how the Bible talks about the Bible. No, it's talking about feasting on the essential nutritional truth of Scripture.

## ANCIENT TRUTH IN THE DIGITAL AGE

I love my old Bible. I really do. For me, nothing can replace that feel of worn leather and the smell of its yellowing pages. That thing is like a journal of my life, with marks and notes all over the place. But the fact is, I'm now "old school," one of the last of the Baby Boomers from post-World War II. Our kids? They are "Gen X" and "Millennials." To them, old leatherbound books look like . . . well, old leatherbound books. My kids are about computer games, smartphone apps, and Google searches. Thankfully, God is too.

Remember, it's not the physical pages of the Bible that are important. It's the words of Scripture on them that bring life. In the digital information age, God is opening up stunning new ways for us to experience His words without ever even opening a paperbound book. Hundreds of apps and programs are giving us access to the truths of Scripture like never before. You might think that computers, tablets, and smartphones are distracting your kids from God, but God can use them to launch your kids into a relevant encounter with truth using the mediums they love. Let me give you just three great resources to explore:

### www.YouVersion.com

This Bible app was created by my friends at LifeChurch.tv, who wanted to attract younger people. They knew they needed both to be technically advanced and offer truth to people for free. Today the YouVersion Bible is available in 2600 versions in more than 1700 languages and has been downloaded more than 500 million times.

### www.BlueLetterBible.org

What used to take me hours of research in a seminary library can now be accomplished in a few seconds by anyone with a pulse and an internet connection. Websites like www.BlueLetterBible.org give us instant access to an insane amount of research, commentaries, and study tools.

Want to know the Greek translation of "love" in John 3:16? Click!

Want to know the Hebrew verb tense in Deuteronomy 6:5? Click!

What to compare four different English translations side by side? Click!

Want to know what a dozen really smart guys said about Genesis 1:1? Click!

Seriously, computers have made intense Bible study so easy that those of us who grew up in the old school are pretty convinced it is cheating.

**www.GloBible.com**

You really have to experience this one to understand how cool it is. By focusing on the truth of Scripture through different "lenses," the GloBible empowers you to explore the Bible from multiple points of view all at once. This amazing program is highly visual and interactive and continues to morph as new versions are released. It even comes in a free "lite" version that never expires.

Honestly, if you're willing to think outside of the box of the way we used to do it, engaging the Bible with our kids has never been easier or more powerful. Never before has the truth of the Bible been served to the world like it is now. It's all you can eat, it's all free, it's 24/7/365, and your kids will eat it up . . . and so will you.

## BACK AT OUR 'SHAREHOLDERS' MEETING

After gathering my wife and my kids together, I shared my embarrassment and my concerns. Yes, there was a lot of really good stuff happening in our family, I told them, yet we had let the good stuff dominate the best. Cindy and I had created a very strong learning environment in our home when it came to academics, I said. But I had dropped the ball when it came to serving the truth of God's Word to my crew.

My kids were becoming masters at memorizing facts and formulas, but we weren't letting the Word of God richly dwell in our hearts or minds (Colossians 3:16). I told them if we did not choose to holistically honor the Bible, everything else in our lives would fall to subjectivity and average. Yet if we hid the Word of God in our hearts, we would be less likely to sin (Psalm 119:11), and God's Word would light up where we were and where we were going (Psalm 119:105).

So then, I put on my man pants and implemented a plan for mandatory reading of the Scriptures. If my child wanted me to pay for their phone, all I asked was for one verse texted to me from their daily reading. No verse, no cell service. Was it legalistic? No. I made them brush their teeth. I made them look both ways before they crossed the street. I made them eat their vegetables. I made them go to the doctor and get their shots. I made them do their algebra homework.

All this is our responsibility as parents. We are the CEOs and COOs. We control the remote. We control the phones. We can lead them to the Word of God too. I didn't want my kids to think calculus was more important than Scripture. I'm not saying academics aren't important. But when academics and athletics become the required and the Bible becomes an elective, we dishonor Him and His Word. So, I decided to make them memorize God's Word, believing it wasn't just going to be good for them; it was going to be fun for them. I even let them take ownership of the process.

The bottom line is this: God's Word is the determining factor for God's best in our lives. It's the truth that brings power to parenting. If we are not willing to honor this text, then everything else is going to fail. It might not ultimately bomb, but you and your kids will miss out on the best that God has to offer unless you honor His Word. The Bible is the ticket, the real deal. When you make it optional, you'll miss out on His best. God's Word is passionate. Every detail is for you and for me and for our kids.

Why is the Word the determining factor for God's best? Because it is truth *and*, ultimately, it points us to the source of all truth and life—Jesus:

> *"You have never heard his voice nor seen his form, nor does his [the Father's] word dwell in you, for you do not believe*

*the one he sent. You study the Scriptures diligently because you think that in them you have eternal life. These are the very Scriptures that testify about me, yet you refuse to come to me to have life."* —JOHN 5:37-40

*Taste and see that the LORD is good; blessed is the one who takes refuge in him. The lions may grow weak and hungry, but those who seek the LORD lack no good thing.* —PSALM 34:8,10

Let's pray together:

*God,*
*I pray that You would give me a spirit of faithfulness to Your Word, from the beginning of Genesis to the end of Revelation. Help me to prioritize moments in my family, and in my own life, for feasting on Your Word every day. I want to be serious about this deal. I want to honor You. I want to put my weight behind You, Jesus, just as You honor us and put Your weight behind us through the resurrection and the redemptive work of the cross. God, use me to raise up my kids as the next generation that understands and serves the truth of your Word, and Your Son, Jesus, to the world.*
*Amen.*

# A HEART CHECKUP: TRAINING

- Spend some time talking with the Lord about His Word.
- Read and ponder 1 Peter 2:1-9.
- What does it say?
- What does it mean?
- How does it relate to me?
- What do I do about it?
- Read and ponder Hebrews 5:9-14.
- What does it say?
- What does it mean?
- How does it relate to me?
- What do I do about it? [I would suggest including a personal Bible study plan that covers the essentials of the gospel and the promise of the Holy Spirit]

Now, call a "family shareholders meeting." If you want to be fancy, take them out like it's a corporate dinner, or borrow actual office space from someone you know and do it around a real conference table.

- Give them your report.
- Point out all the stuff that's going really well.
- Affirm each of them as a welcome and indispensable part of the family business.
- Read Deuteronomy 6:1-9.
- Have each kid pick out the thing they feel is most important in this passage.

- Brainstorm about how you could apply the following commands in your home:

*These commandments that I give you today are to be on your hearts. Impress them on your children. Talk about them when you sit at home and when you walk along the road, when you lie down and when you get up. Tie them as symbols on your hands and bind them on your foreheads. Write them on the doorframes of your houses and on your gates. —DEUTERONOMY 6:6-9*

- Pray for a while, ask God for His guidance, and go back through and pick out the top ideas that can be implemented right now.
- Ask God to work through your lives by the power of the Holy Spirit to make these things a reality.

## AFTERWORD

# THE HEART OF
# THE GOSPEL

*Jesus said to him, "Today salvation has come to this*
*house, because this man, too, is a son of Abraham. For*
*the Son of Man came to seek and to save the lost."*
—LUKE 19: 9-10

**W**e were just one more typical family in a typical neighborhood, and we fit in just fine. Mom and Dad would sometimes put us on the church bus when we were little, and a couple times a year (Christmas and Easter), they would wash us and dress us up and try to keep us from fidgeting while the preacher talked, and our feet stuck out straight over the edge of the pew. But that was about it. We were American, middle-class, and we were comfortable.

But when I was nine, somebody came into our lives who messed up our contented, undisturbed life of ease . . . and she did it in her home.

Mrs. Plumlee started having us over for dinner. She was an amputee with only one leg and couldn't use a prosthesis much, so most of the time, she was on crutches, but she was definitely walking well with Christ. She would cook up this spread and lay it out, and we would chow down—Norman Rockwell stuff. But there was more to it than that, much more.

Mrs. Plumlee knew that we needed to eat something more than the great meatloaf and potatoes. She used her home to invite us to drink living water and eat the bread of life. She was just passing on the invitation she had accepted from Jesus—so we could let Him into our house and dine with Him. She just kept feeding us and inviting us to come to church. We just kept on eating, but one Sunday, we took her up on her invitation . . . and that changed everything.

My mom was already a Christian, but getting into church lit her fire again, and she started to live for Jesus in new ways. Then, my brother got saved. Then I got saved. Then my sister prayed to receive Christ. Then I remember my dad sitting at a table with the pastor, and he prayed to receive Christ right there at our table when he was thirty-nine. He was baptized the following Sunday.

One by one, that's how we all came to know Christ. It's crazy to think about it, really. It's like we were all stacked up like a big row of dominoes ready to tumble over into a world of faith. For all I know, we could still be sitting there, stacked up and ready. It was Martha Plumlee that gave us the flick, starting the chain reaction that has transformed our lives on earth and changed the trajectory of our eternity.

I shudder when I think about what our lives would be like if she hadn't invited us and modeled something of God's love. And it all began in her home. Just as Jesus invited Himself to Zacchaeus's house because He came "to seek and save the lost" (Luke 19:10), He wants to come to our homes so we might experience His life-changing love and become places where others encounter it too.

When the home is healthy, when marriages are healthy, and families are healthy, God's church is going to be healthy too. It becomes a place of ministry with food prepared—living bread and life-giving water—ready to be served to guests who are desperate for rescue.

The greatest commands are that we love God with all we have and that we love our neighbors as ourselves. Opening our hearts to Him, we allow His love to fill our hearts. We let the Holy Spirit renew our hearts. We invite Him to remove any blockages, so that His love may flow freely through us to others.

Jesus is the vine. We are the branches. If we abide in His love, we will bear much fruit . . . fruit that can be served to others.

He sacrificed so we can serve.

He fed us so we can feed others.

He loved us so we can love.

When I realized all this, I was sitting at a table with my dad. Over a McDonald's sausage and egg McMuffin, I shared my call to ministry.

His response: "Go be the next Billy Graham, son."

# GOING FURTHER

## Romance Uncensored!

As I hope you've discovered in the pages of this book, I'm excited about marriage—both how fulfilling it can be personally and how it's such a great illustration and example of the good news of the kingdom.

If you'd like to hear more about what Cindy and I have learned about marriage, you can join us at one of our Romance Uncensored events. We get real about it all and have a lot of fun in the process.

Or maybe instead of attending a Romance Uncensored event, you'd like to host one in your church or your community? If so, we would love to consider coming and sharing.

To find out more, go to www.romanceuncensored.com, or email us at info@romanceuncensored.com.

**YouTube:** Romance Uncensored
**Instagram:** @romanceuncensored

# ABOUT THE AUTHOR

Shannon O'Dell is Senior Pastor of 1,200-member Brand New Church in Bergman, Arkansas (population 400), which has satellite campuses in Farmington, and Calico Rock. He is the author of *Transforming Church in Rural America: Breaking all the Rurals*.

Shannon and his wife, Cindy, have been married for almost 30 years and have four children (Anna, Evan, Sara, and K.J) and one grandson. When he is not active in ministry, he enjoys spending time with his family and hunting.

Learn more about Brand New Church and find more of Shannon's teaching at www.brandnewchurch.com and www.shannonodell.com.

**FOLLOW SHANNON ON:**
**Facebook:** ShannonBNC
**Instagram:** @Shannondell
**Twitter:** @shannonodell

# APPENDIX A

## A Marriage Creed

If you want a daily action guide for your marriage, you'll find a 44-point plan in Ephesians 4:23-5:33. Focus on one of these each day over the next six weeks and see how God might work in you and in your marriage as a result.

1) Renew your thoughts and attitudes (4:23)
2) Stop telling lies (v.25)
3) Don't let anger control you (v.26)
4) Don't go to bed mad (v.26)
5) Be aware that anger props the door open for the devil (v.27)
6) Work hard (v.28)
7) Give generously (v.29)
8) Don't cuss (v.29)
9) Don't use abusive words (v.29)
10) Let everything you say be good, helpful, encouraging (v.29)

11) Don't hurt the Holy Spirit by the way you live (v.30)
12) Get rid of all bitterness, rage, anger, harsh words, slander (v.31)
13) Be kind (v.32)
14) Be tenderhearted (v.32)
15) Forgive like Jesus (v.33)
16) Mimic God in everything (5:1)
17) Live filled with love (v.2)
18) Follow Christ's example (v.2)
19) No fooling around (v.3)
20) Don't be greedy (v.3)
21) No obscene stories/jokes (v.4)
22) Be thankful (v.4)
23) Remove the wrong friends (v.6)
24) Don't hang with the wrong people (v.7)
25) Be light (v.8)
26) Make a list of what pleases God (v.10)
27) Expose worthless stuff and get rid of it (v.12)
28) Shine your light (vv.12-14)
29) Don't live like a fool (v.15)
30) Make the most of every opportunity (v.16)
31) Don't act thoughtlessly (v.17)
32) Don't drink too much (v.18)
33) Worship in song with your spouse (v.19)
34) Give thanks for everything (v.20)
35) Submit to one another (v.21)
36) Submit to your husband (v.22)

37) Submit to your wife by loving her as much as Christ loves His bride (the church) (v.24)
38) Read/pray over her (v26)
39) Present her to God glorious (v.27)
40) Love her more than yourself (v.28)
41) Care for her as Christ cares for His church (v.29)
42) Become one (v.31)
43) Love your wife like Jesus (v.33)
44) Respect your husband (v.38)